Masterpieces of Morland (1911)

ISBN-13 : 978-1512340150
ISBN-10 : 1512340154

Notice

This documentary study use historic, archived documents.

Because of this, some pages may look blurry or low quality.

Still are included in this book because they have

high value from critical, documentary, historical,

informative and journalistic point of view .

Dtp
and
visual art

Iacob Adrian

THE
MASTERPIECES
OF
MORLAND

(1763-1804)

Sixty reproductions of photographs from the original paintings, affording examples of the different characteristics of the Artist's work

Author statement

This is a series of art books .

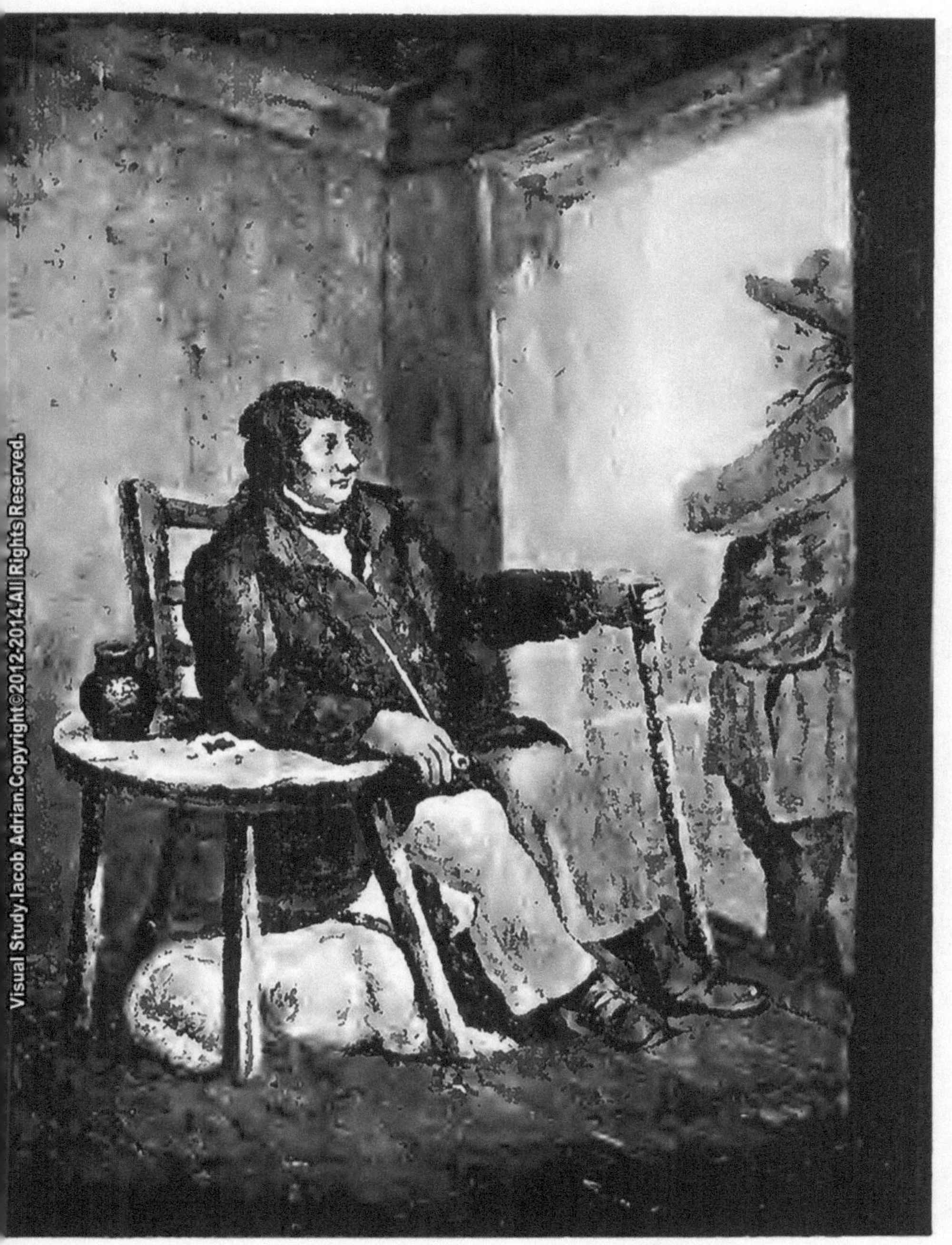

THE ARTIST AND A FRIEND L'ARTISTE ET UN AMI

DER MALER UND EIN FREUND

(Mrs. F. Abbiss Phillips, Stoke d'Abernon)

H. Hyatt, Photo.

This little Book conveys the greetings of

....

to

....

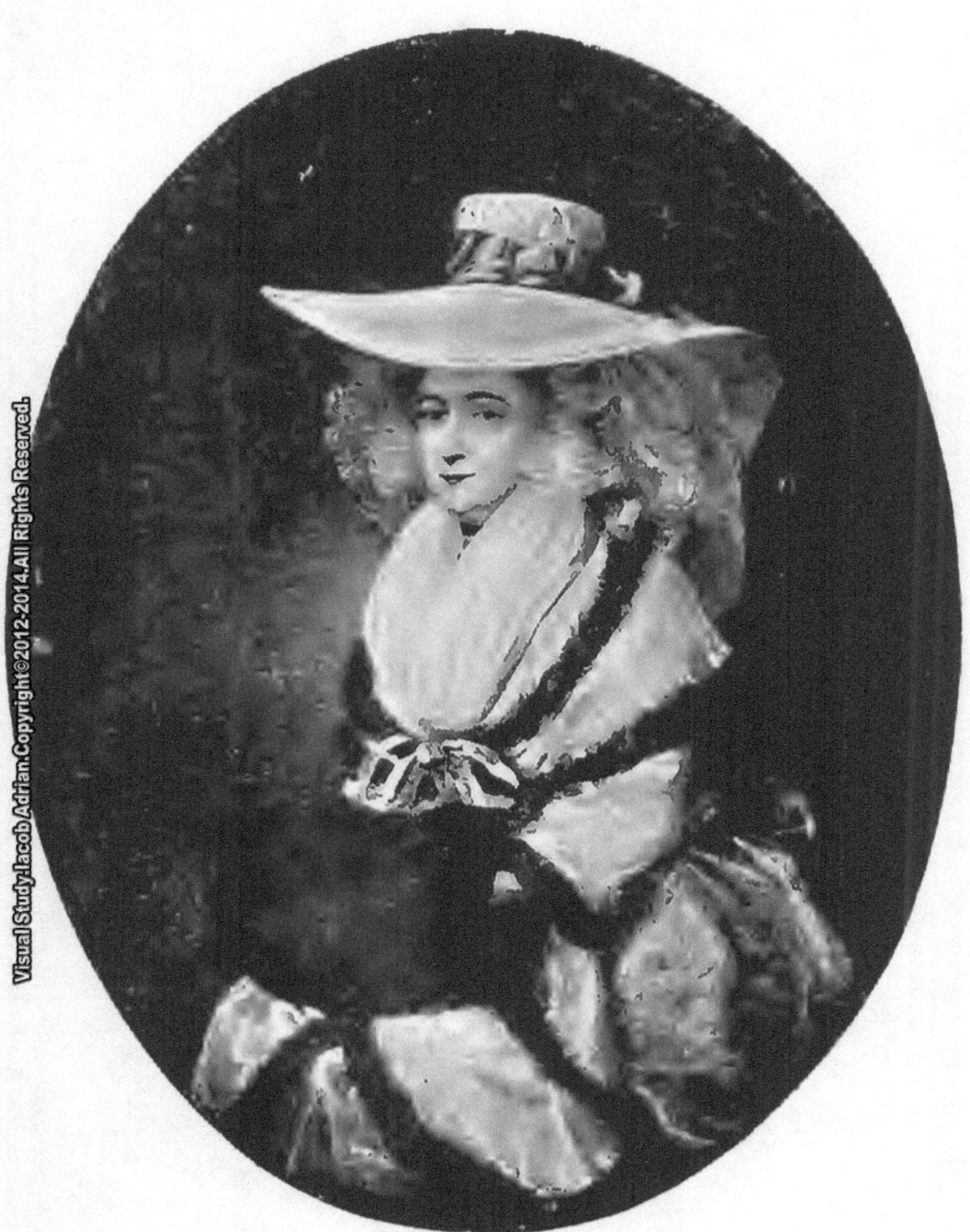

MRS. JORDAN

(Mrs. F. Abbiss Phillips, Stoke d'Abernon)

H. Hyatt, Photo.

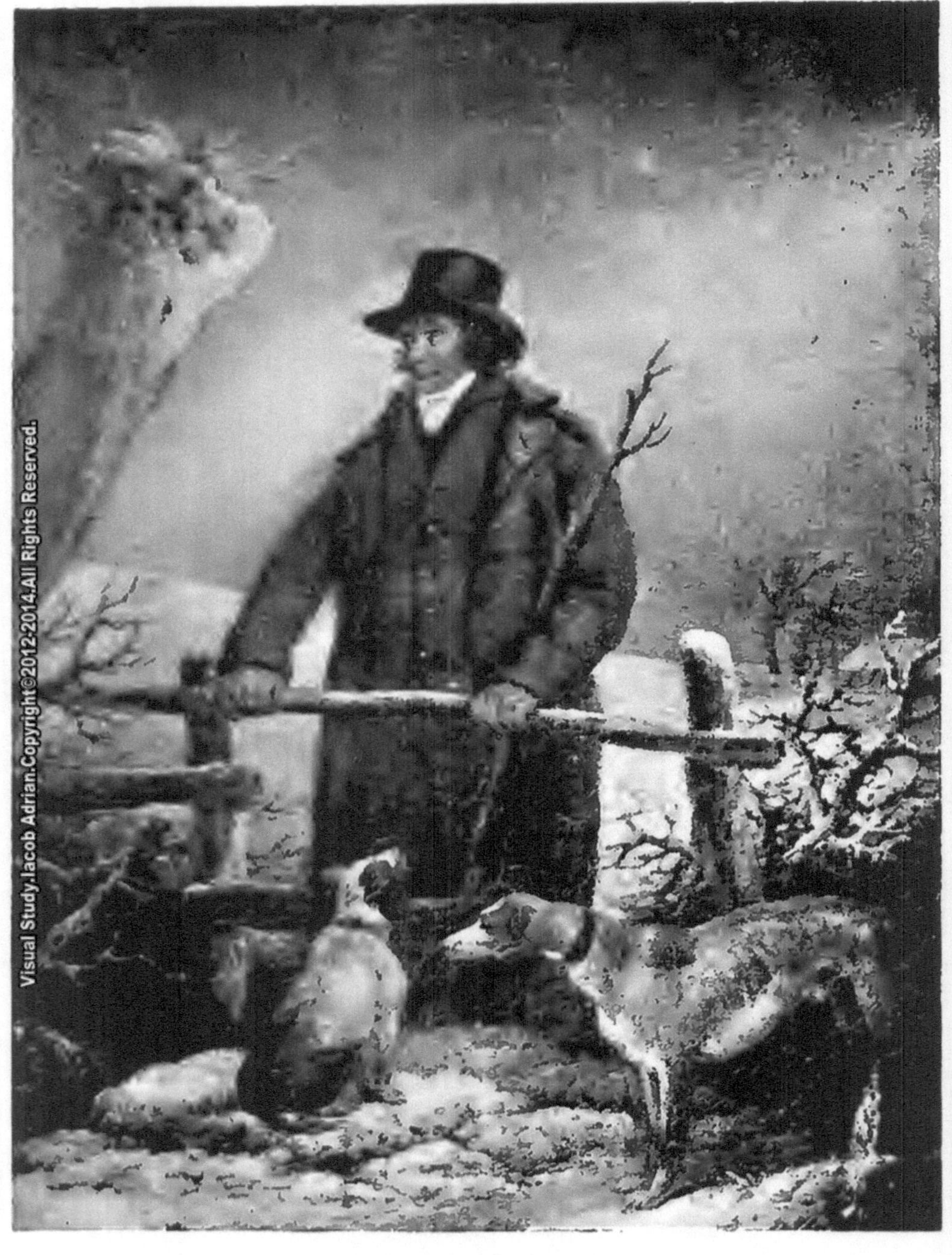

MORLAND'S SERVANT, SIMPSON

SIMPSON, DOMESTIQUE DE MORLAND

SIMPSON, MORLANDS DIENER

(*Mrs. F. Abbiss Phillips, Stoke d'Abernon*)

J. Caswall Smith, Photo.

3

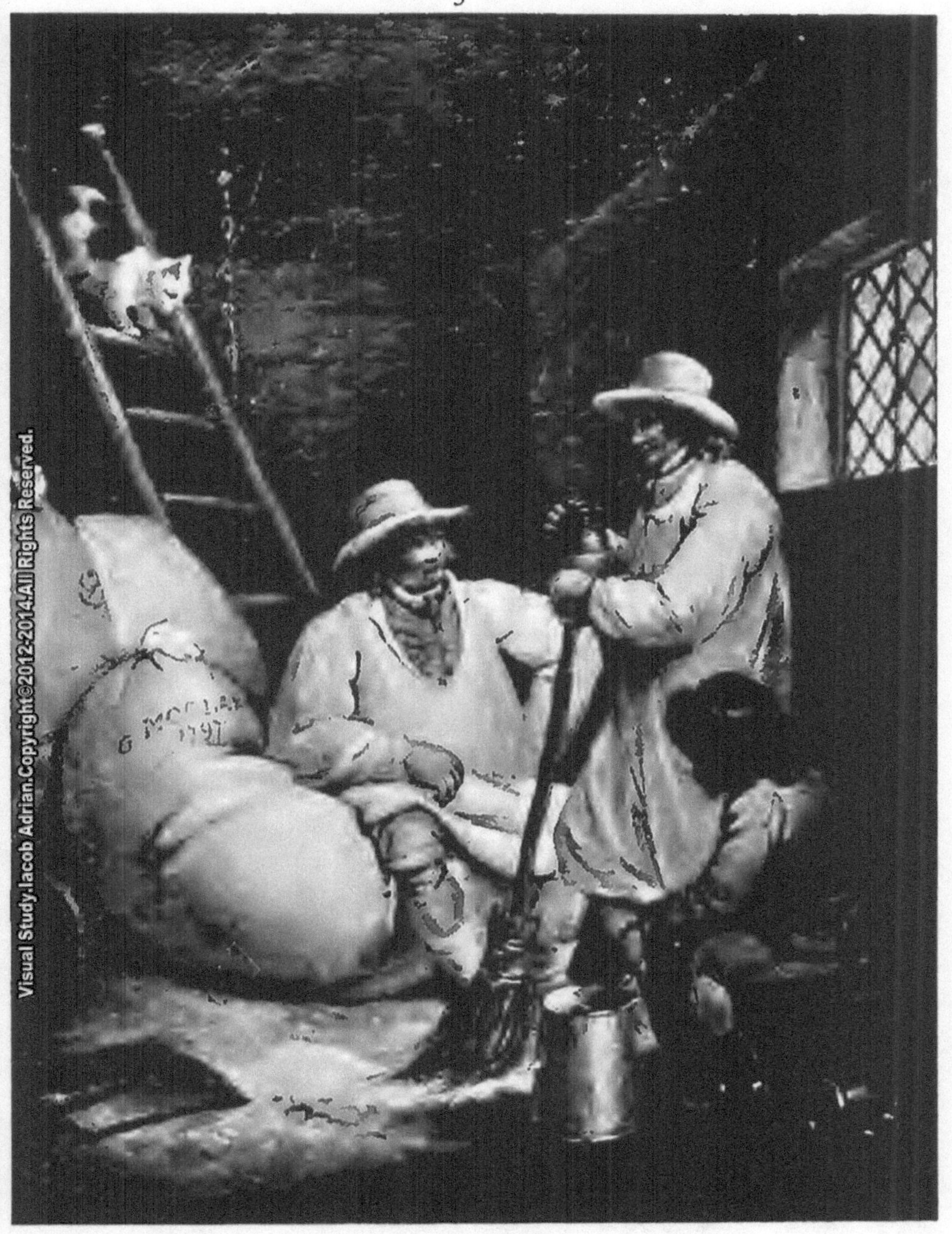

THE MILLER AND HIS MEN LE MEUNIER ET SES GARÇONS

DER MÜLLER UND SEINE GESELLEN

(*Mrs. F. Abbiss Phillips, Stoke d'Abernon*)

H. Hyatt, Photo.

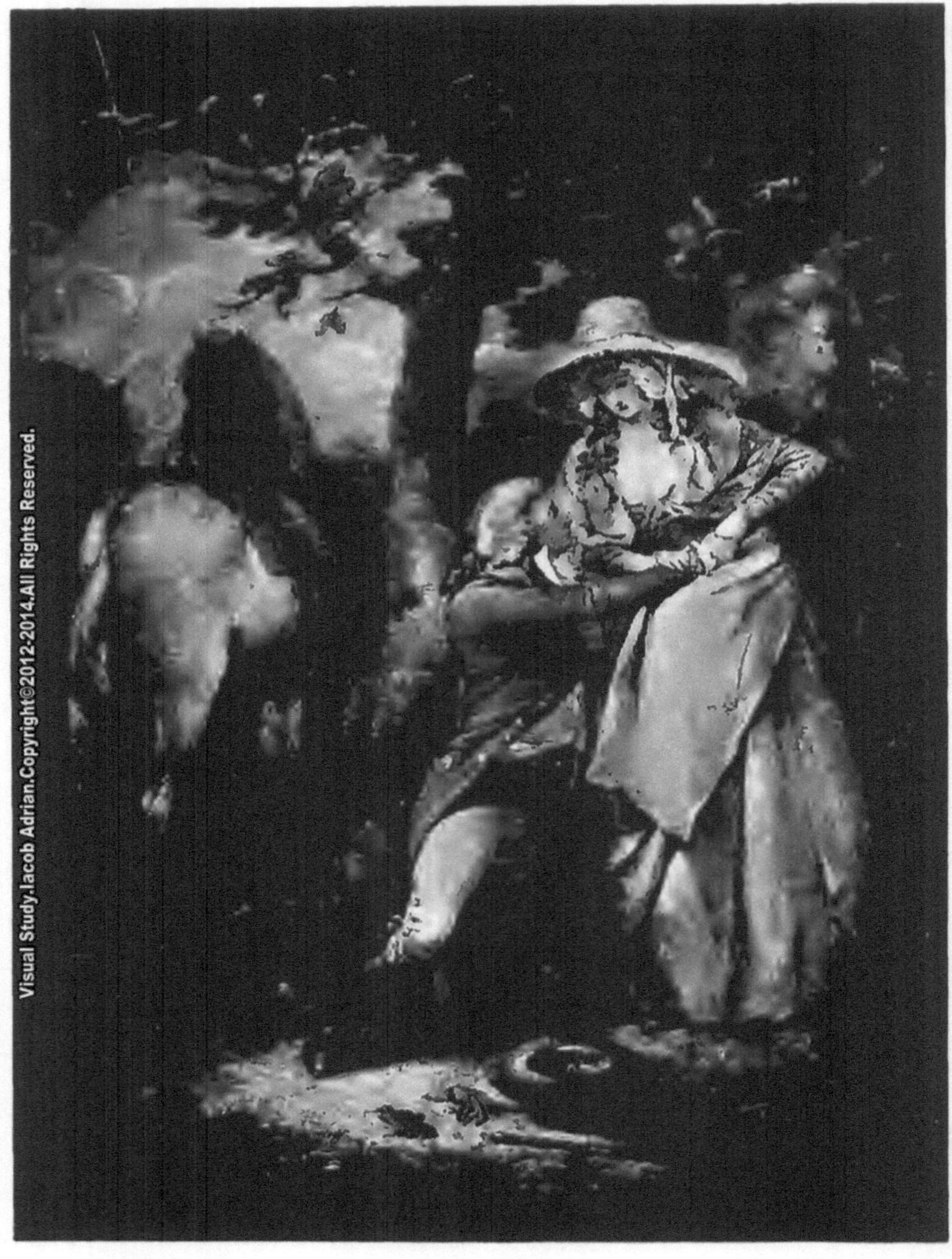

SQUIRE THORNHILL AND OLIVIA

LE CHEVALIER THORNHILL ET OLIVIA

DER JUNKER THORNHILL UND OLIVIA

(Mr. A. M. Byers, Pittsburg)

Braun, Clément et Cie, Photo.

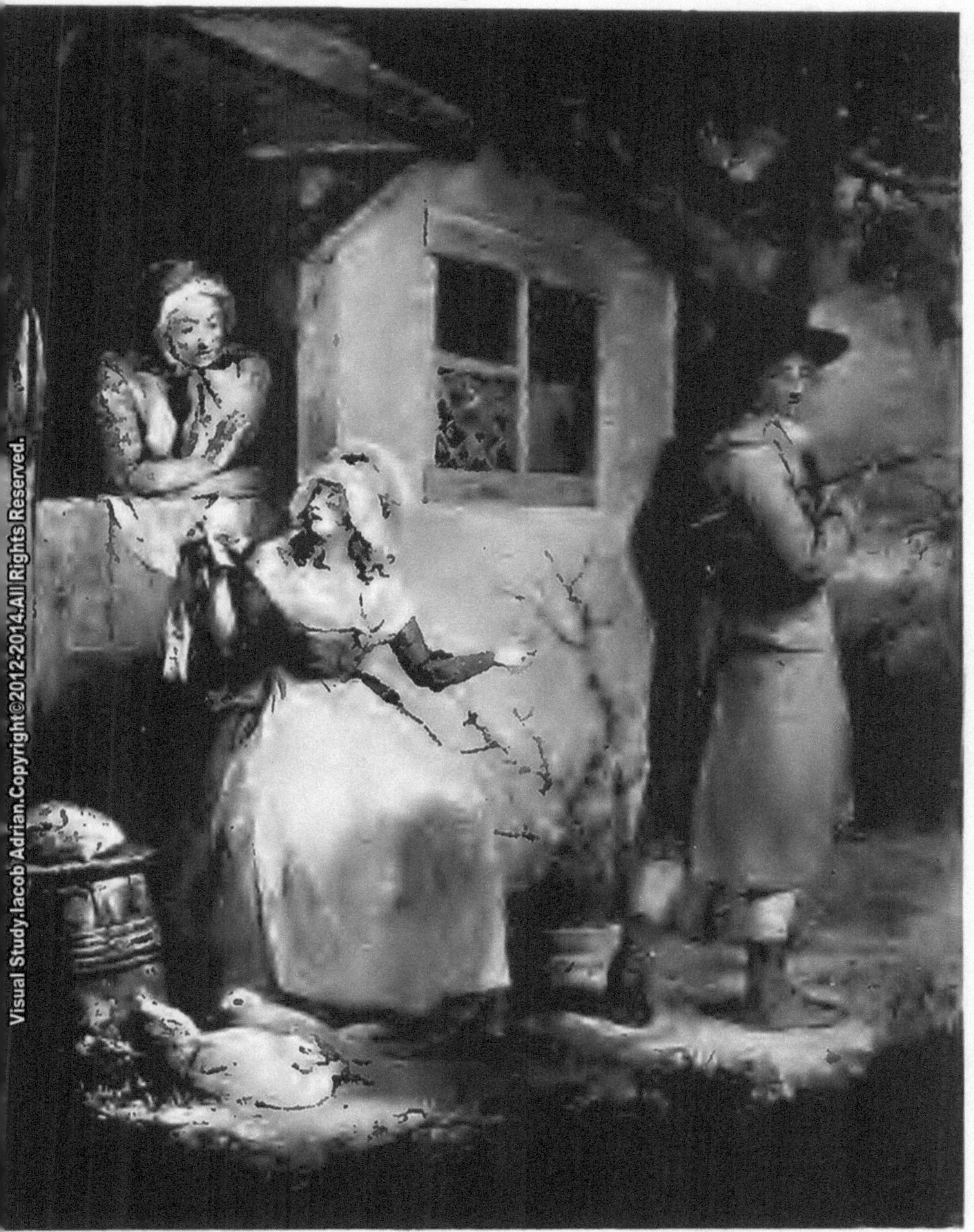

VALENTINE'S DAY OR JOHNNY GOING TO THE FAIR

LE JOUR DE ST VALENTIN

VALENTINSTAG

(*Victoria and Albert Museum, South Kensington*)

J. Caswall Smith, Photo.

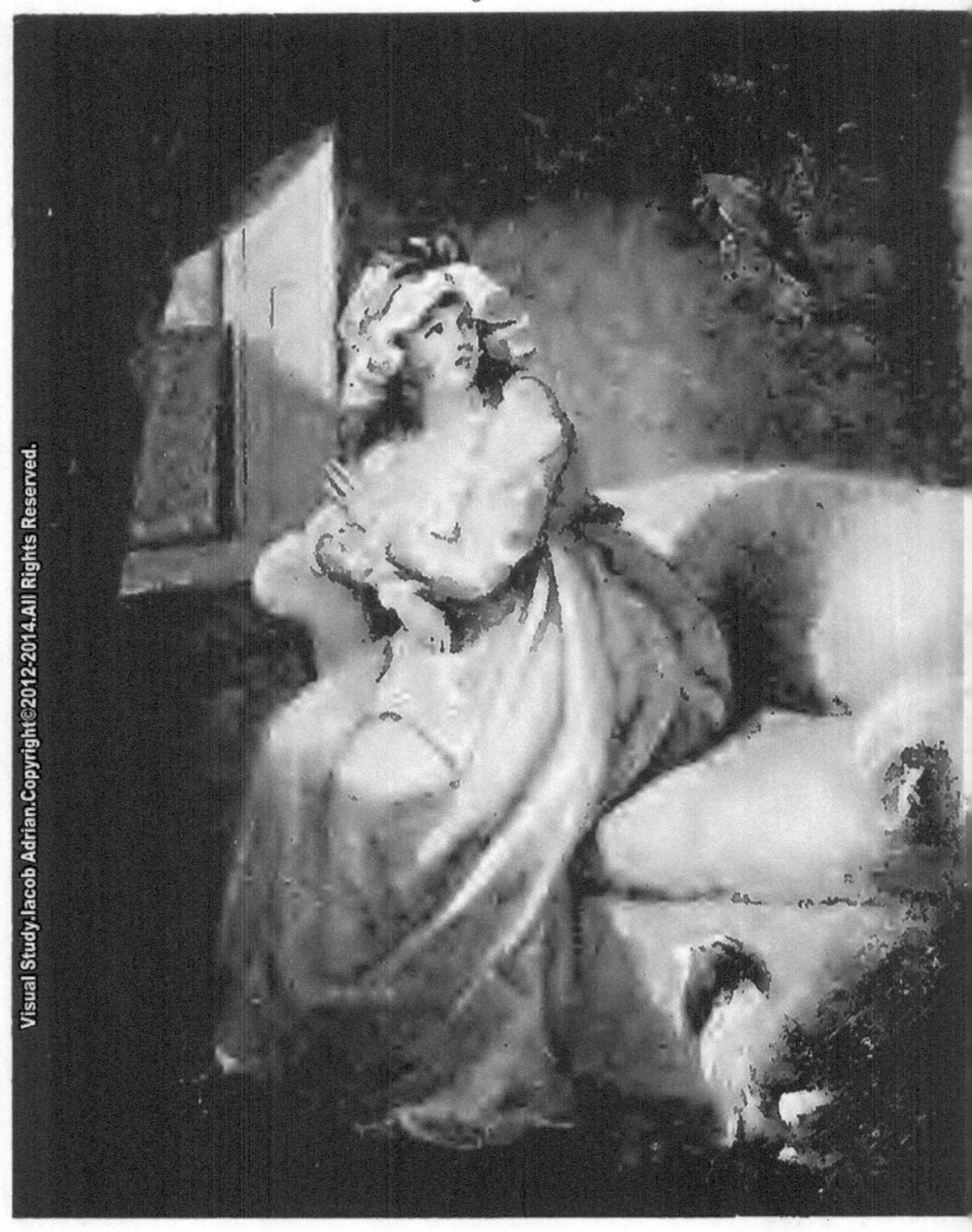

THE DISCONSOLATE AND HER PARROT

LA DÉSOLÉE ET SON PERROQUET

DIE UNTRÖSTLICHE UND IHR PAPAGEI

(*Mrs. F. Abbiss Phillips, Stoke d'Abernon*)

J. Caswall Smith, Photo.

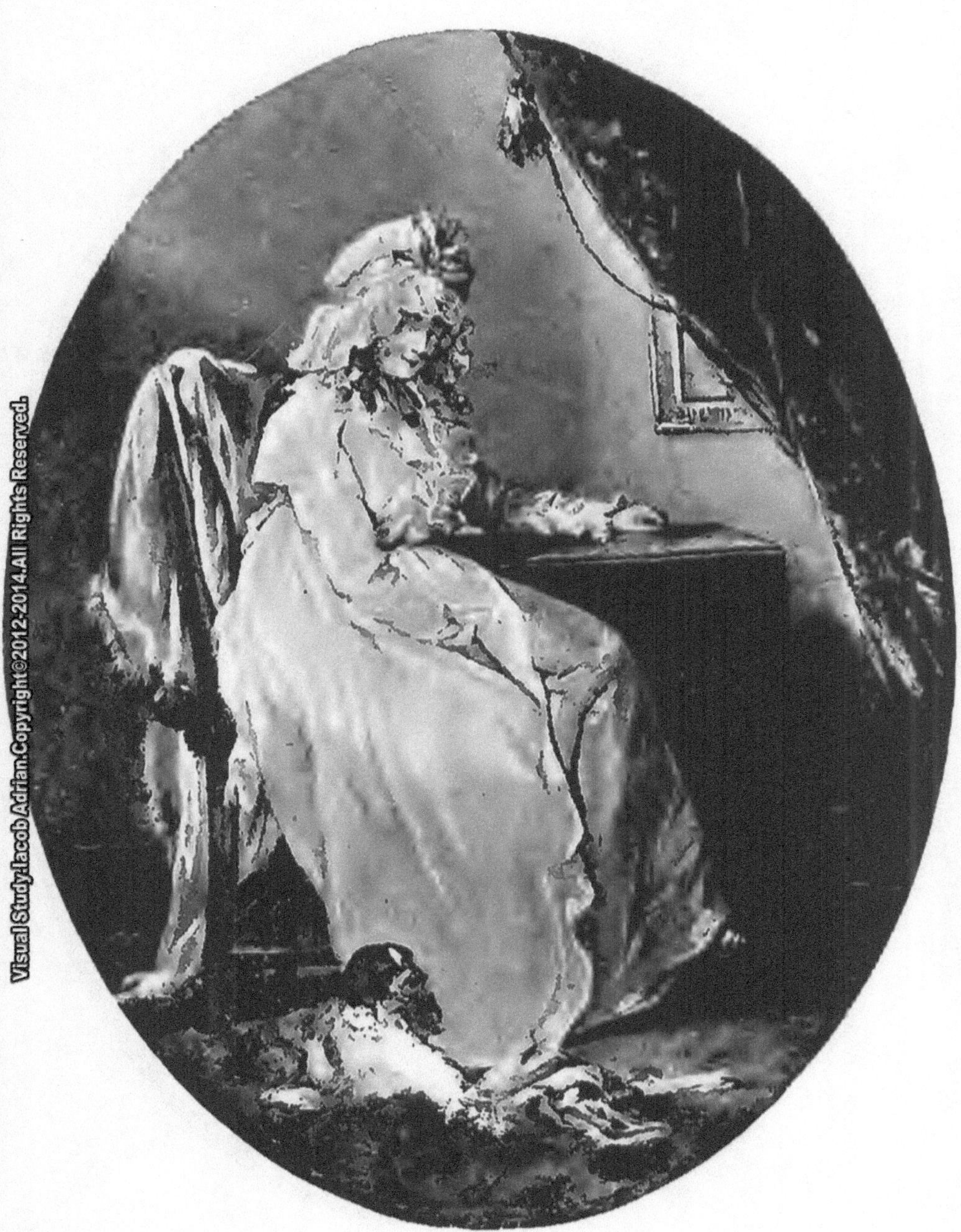

IDLENESS DIE TRÄGHEIT LA PARESSE

(Lord Glenconner, London)

H. Hyatt, Photo.

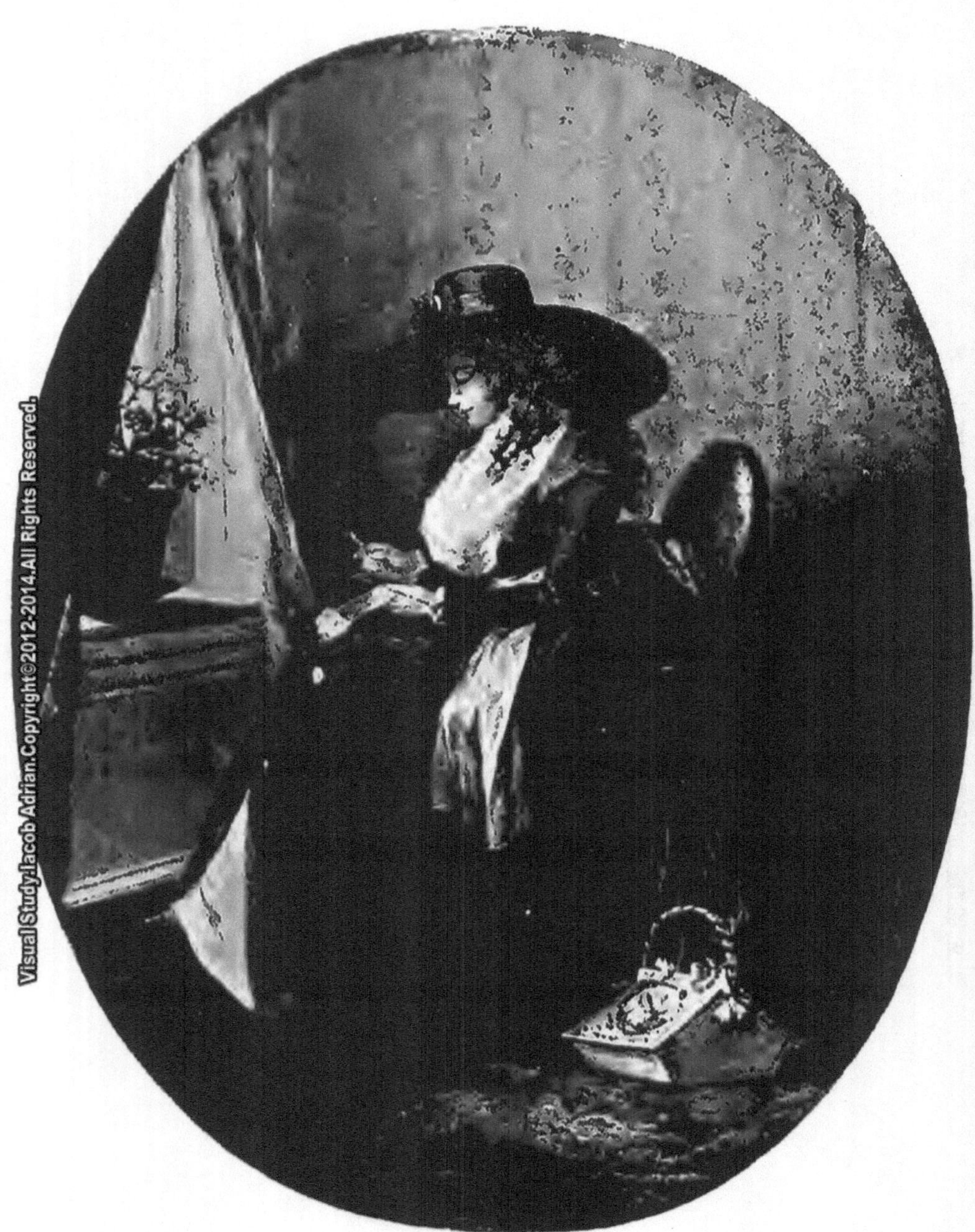

DILIGENCE DER FLEISS L'ASSIDUITÉ

(Lord Glenconner, London)

H. Hyatt, Photo.

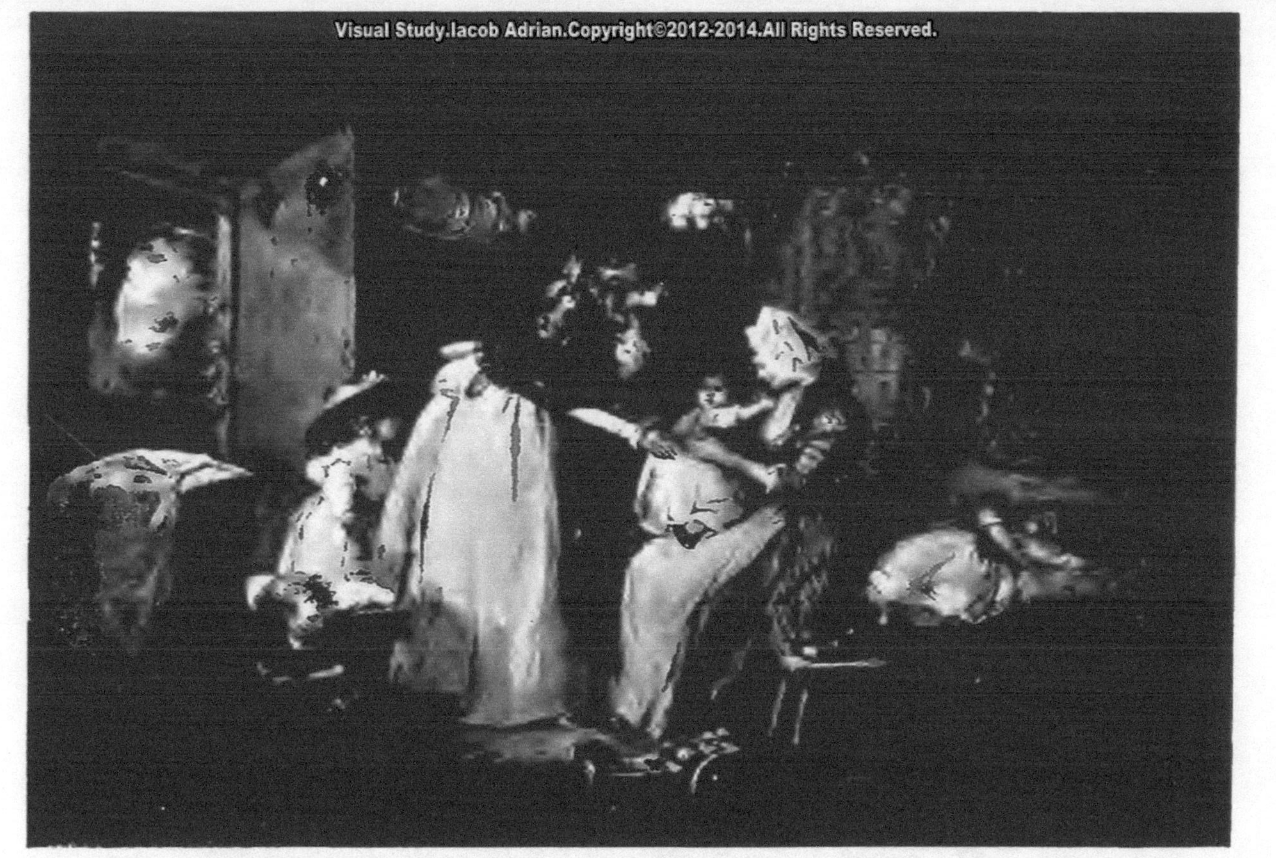

The Visit to the Child at Nurse La Visite a l'Enfant en Nourrice

Der Besuch des Kindes bei der Amme

(M. Ch. Sedelmeyer, Paris) *Braun, Clément et Cie, Photo.*

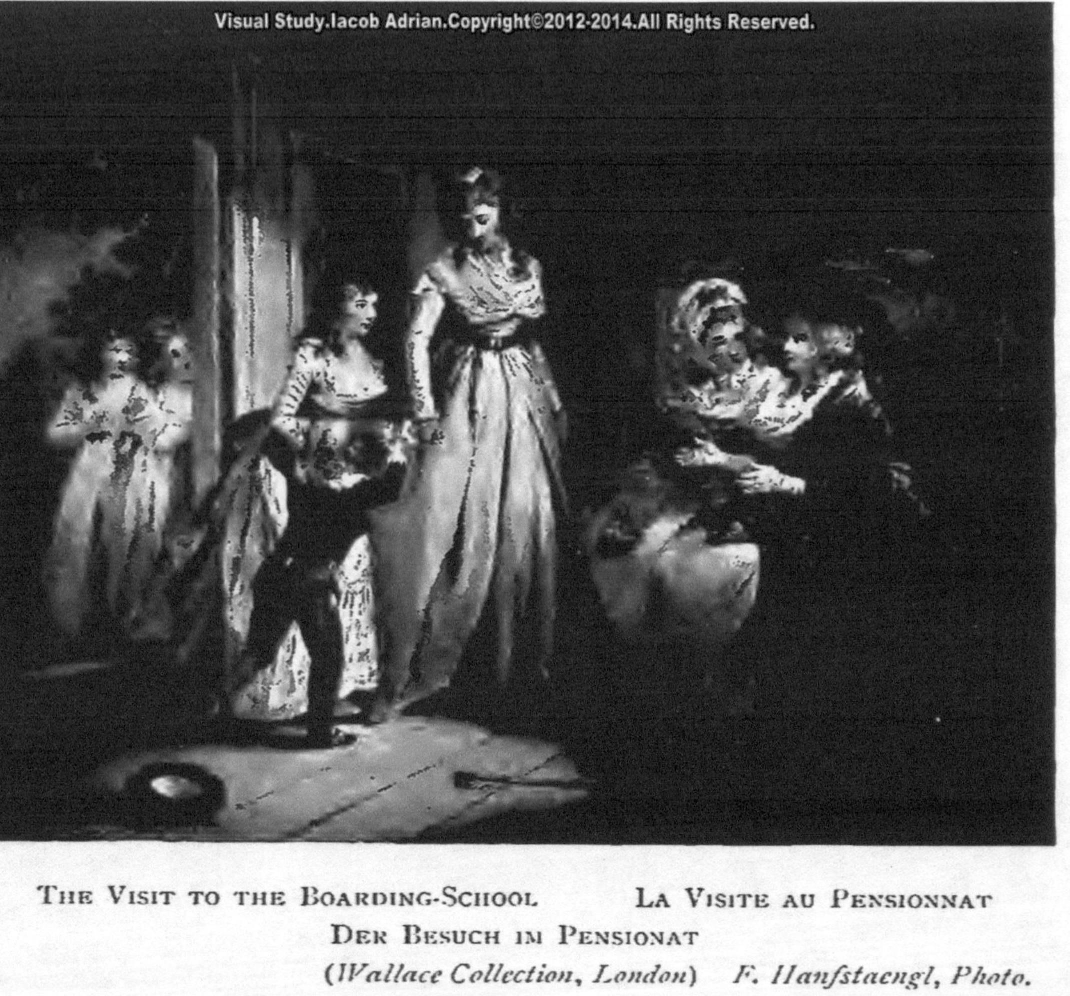

THE VISIT TO THE BOARDING-SCHOOL LA VISITE AU PENSIONNAT

DER BESUCH IM PENSIONAT

(Wallace Collection, London) *F. Hanfstaengl, Photo.*

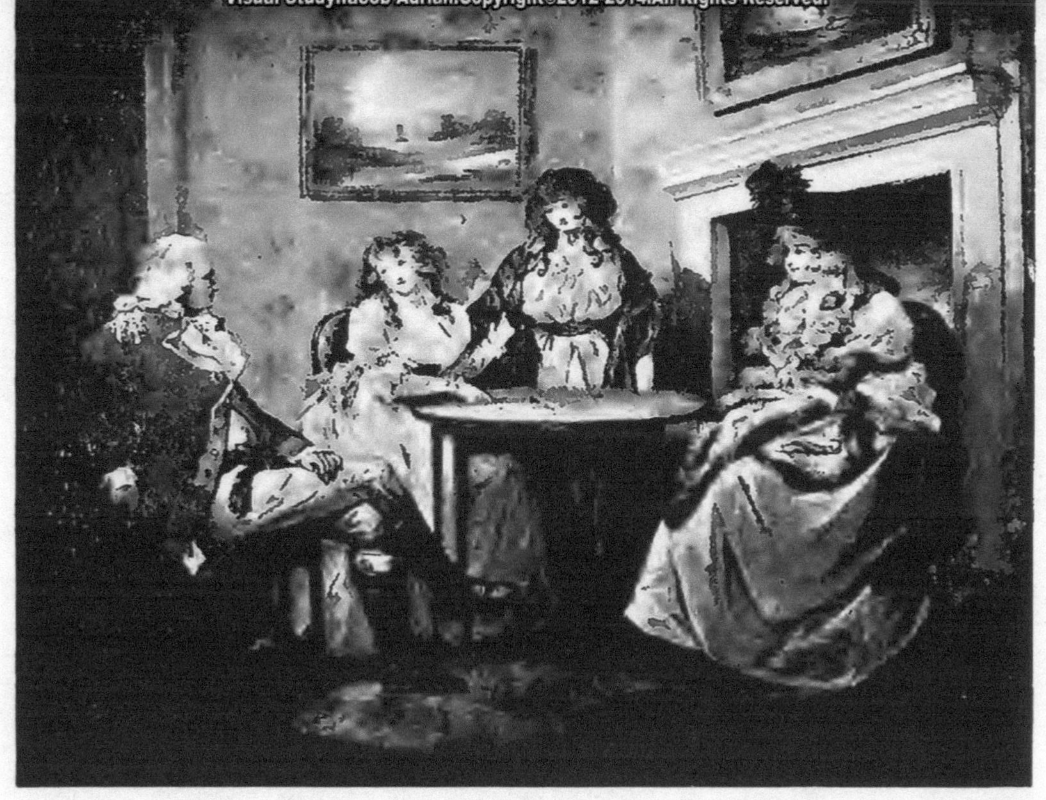

THE FORTUNE-TELLER LA DISEUSE DE BONNE AVENTURE

DIE WAHRSAGERIN

(*National Gallery, London*)

W. A. Mansell & Co., Photo.

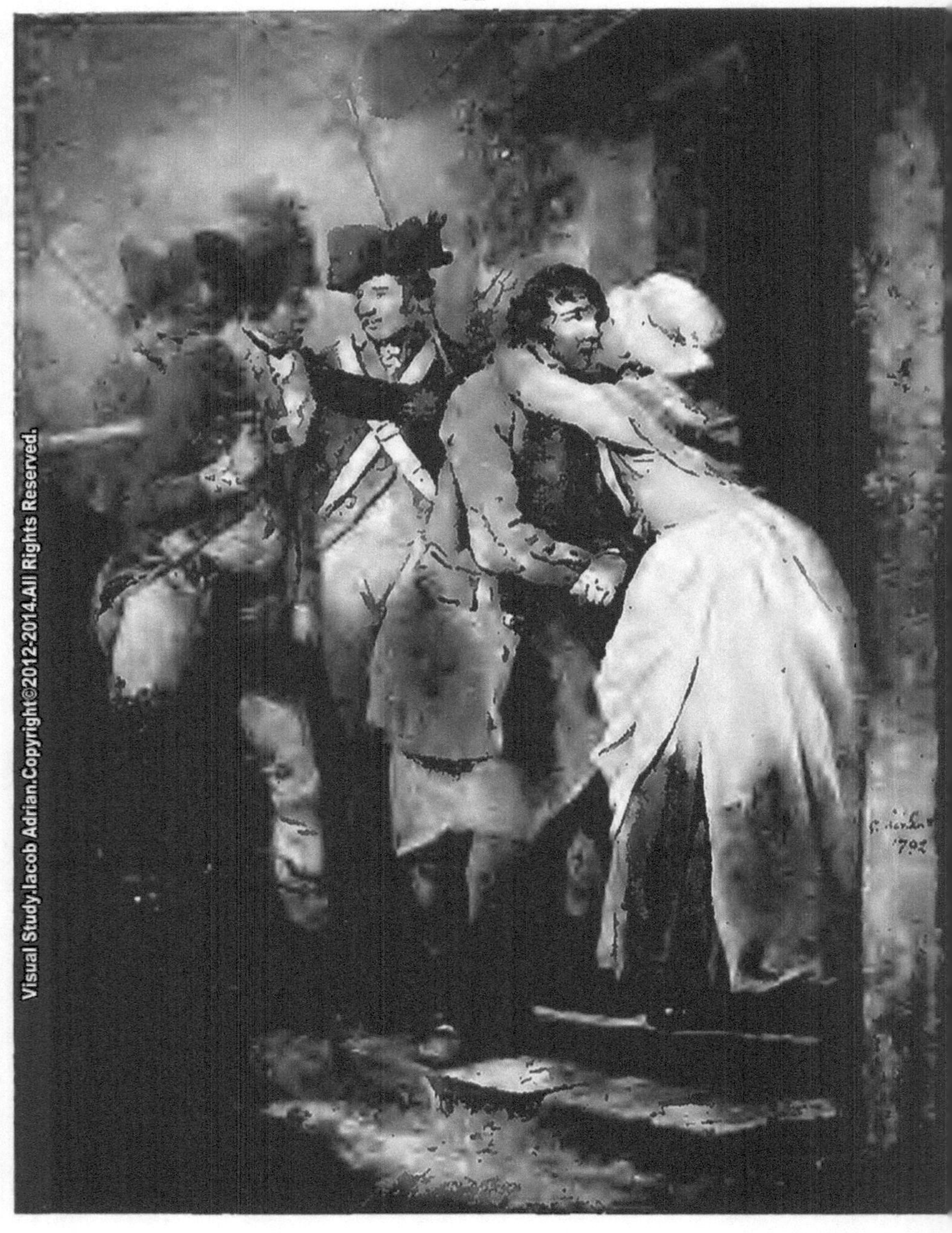

THE DESERTER'S FAREWELL L'ADIEU DU DÉSERTEUR

DAS LEBEWOHL DES DESERTEURS

(*Sir Walter Gilbey, Bart., Elsenham Hall*)

J. Caswall Smith, Photo.

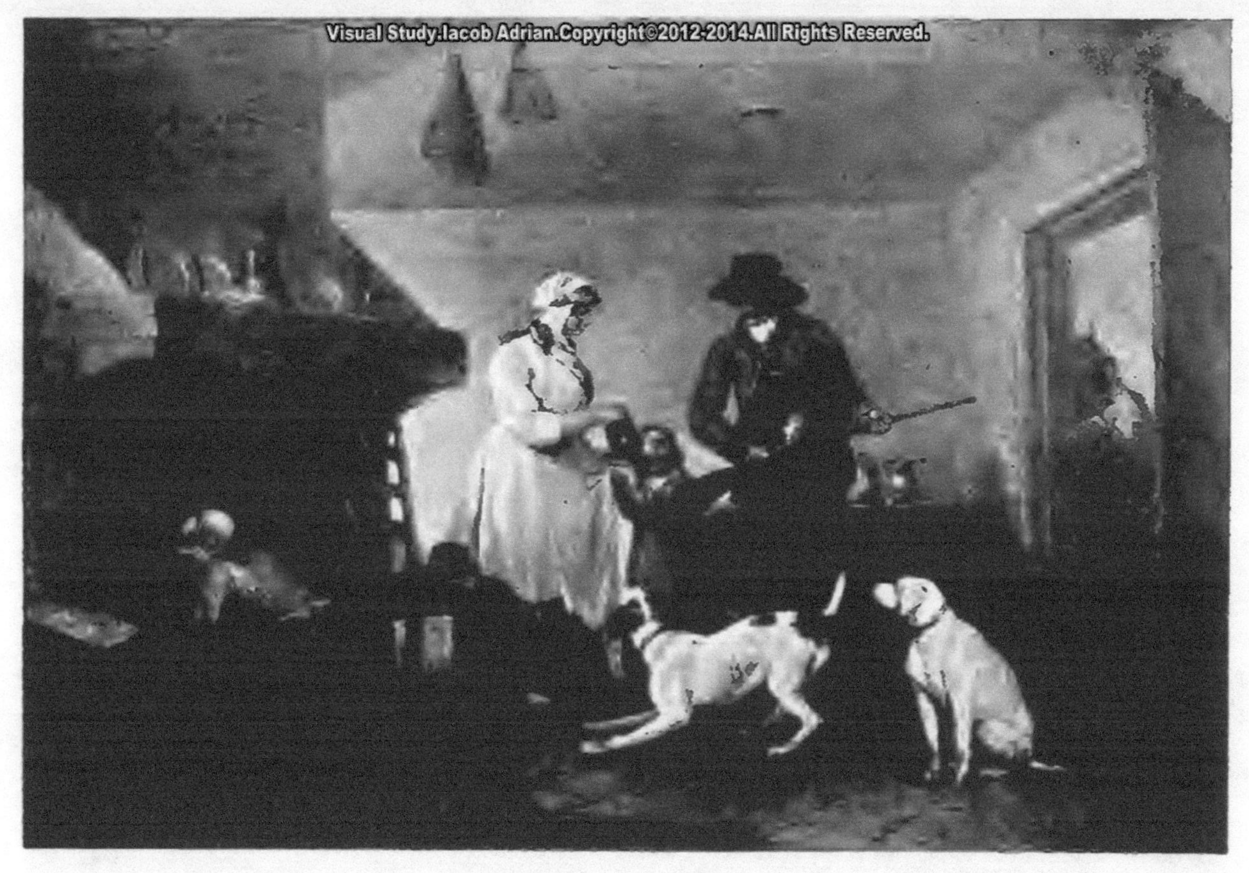

INNOCENCE ALARMED DIE ERSCHROCKENE UNSCHULD L'INNOCENCE EFFRAYÉE

(Sir Walter Gilbey, Bart., Elsenham Hall)

J. Caswall Smith, Photo.

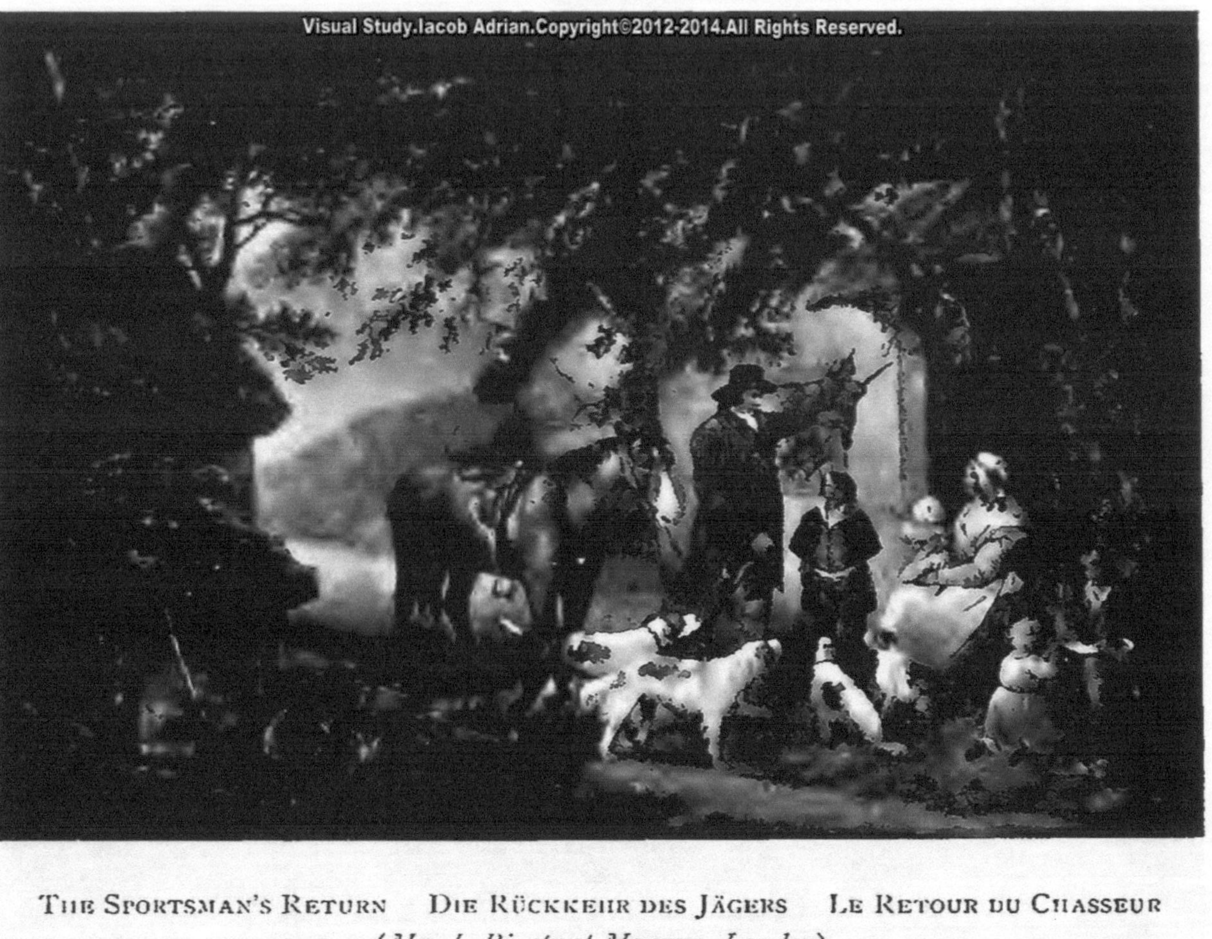

THE SPORTSMAN'S RETURN   DIE RÜCKKEHR DES JÄGERS   LE RETOUR DU CHASSEUR

(Mr. J. Pierpont Morgan, London)

Braun, Clément et Cie. Photo.

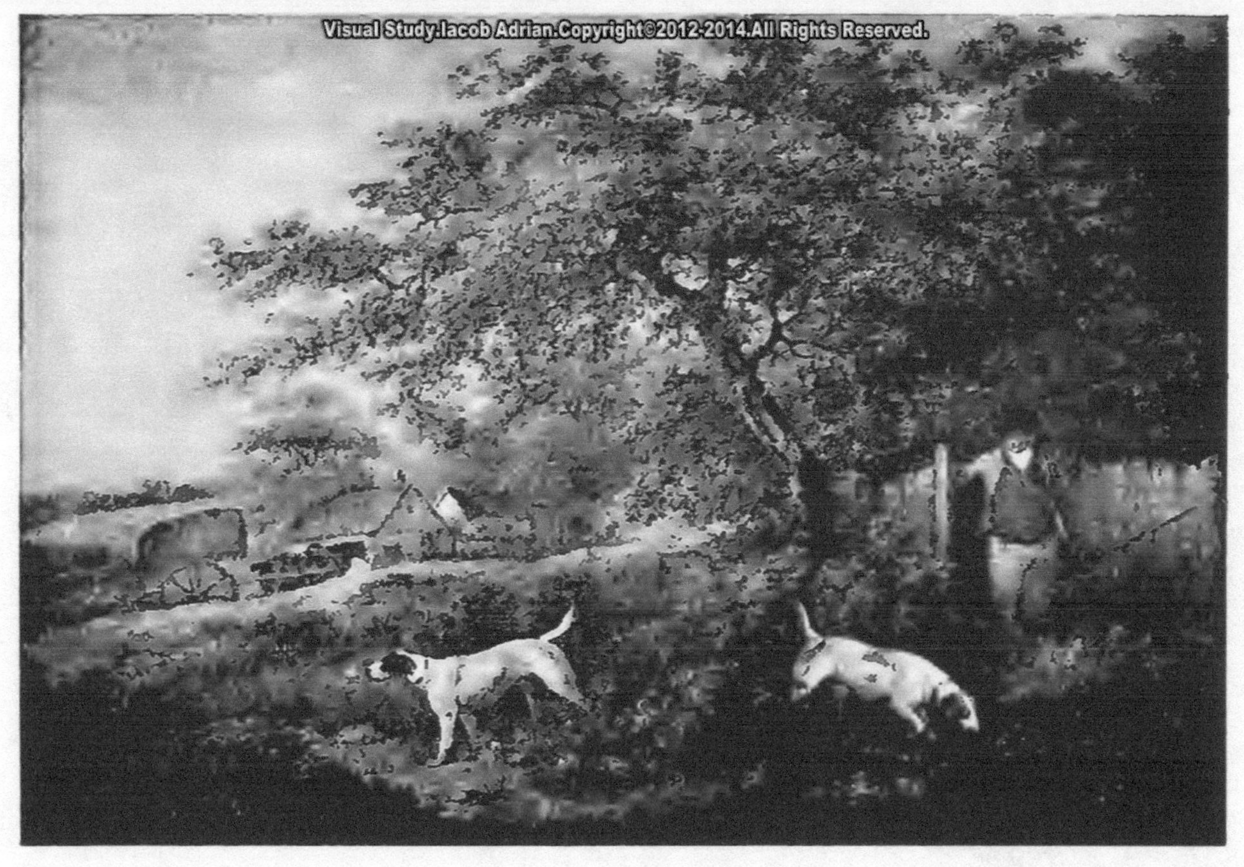

THE FIRST OF SEPTEMBER DER ERSTE SEPTEMBER LE PREMIER SEPTEMBRE

(Mrs. F. Abbiss Phillips, Stoke d'Abernon)

H. Hyatt, Photo.

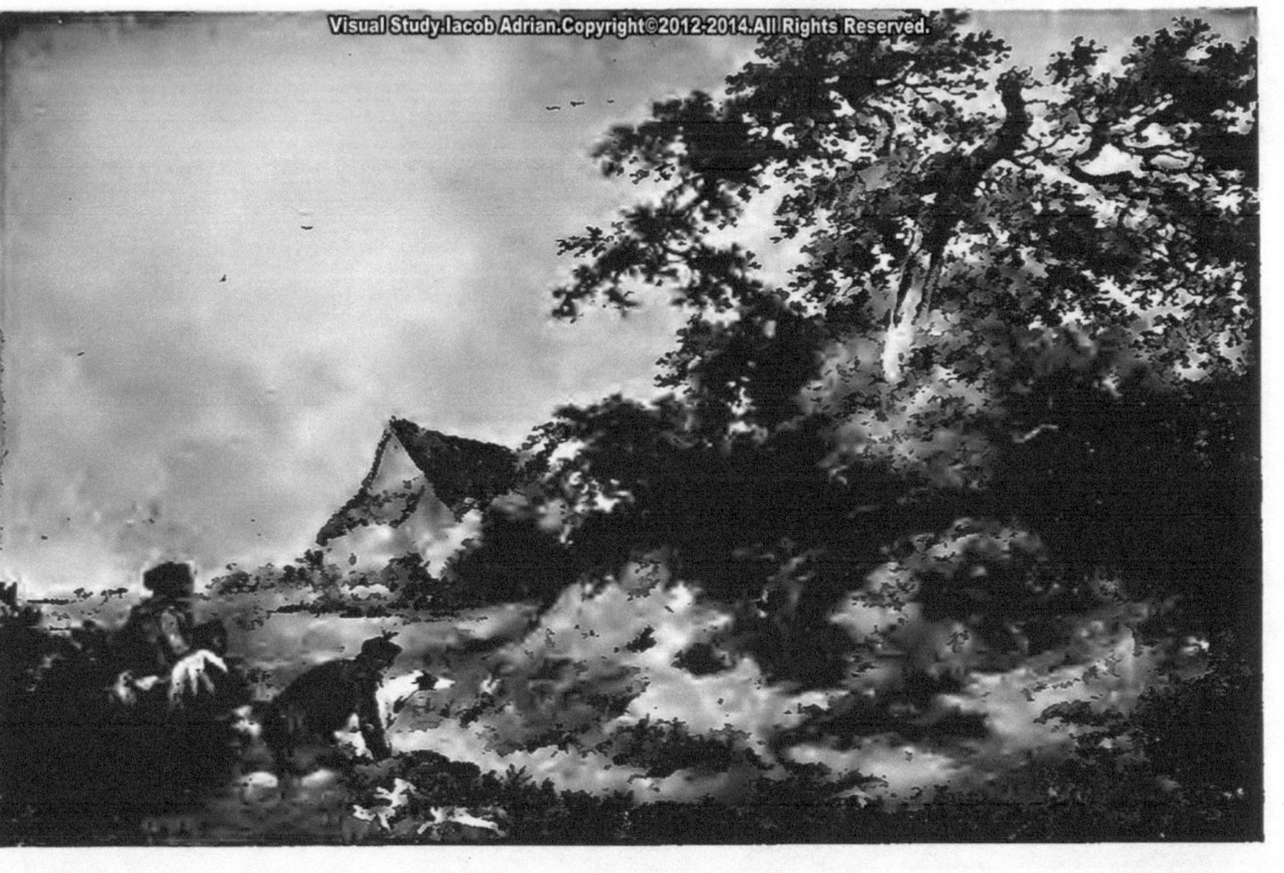

RABBITING — JAGD AUF KANINCHEN — CHASSE AUX LAPINS

(National Gallery, London)

W. A. Mansell & Co , Photo.

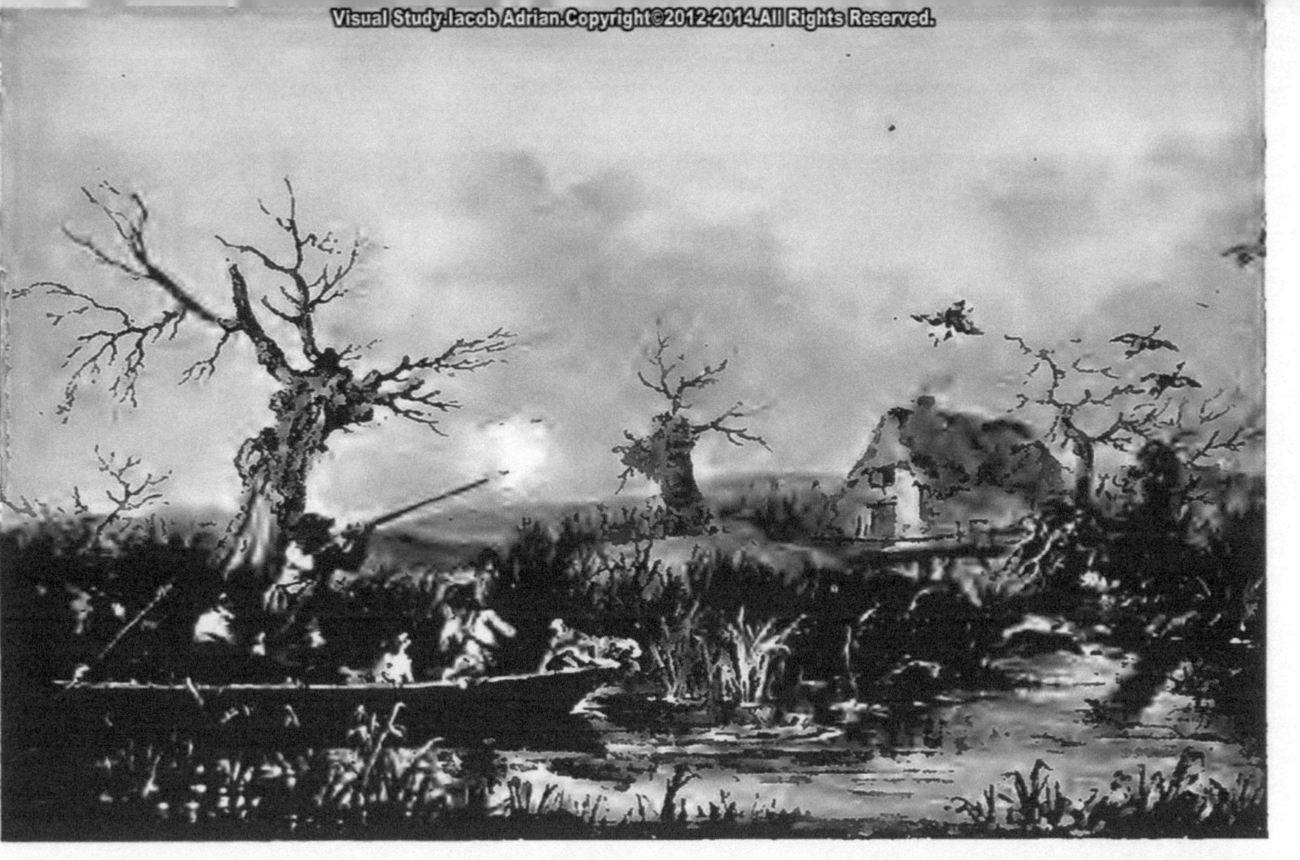

DUCK-SHOOTING   ENTENJAGD   CHASSE AUX CANARDS

(Mr. P. A. B. Widener, Philadelphia)

Braun, Clément et Cie, Photo.

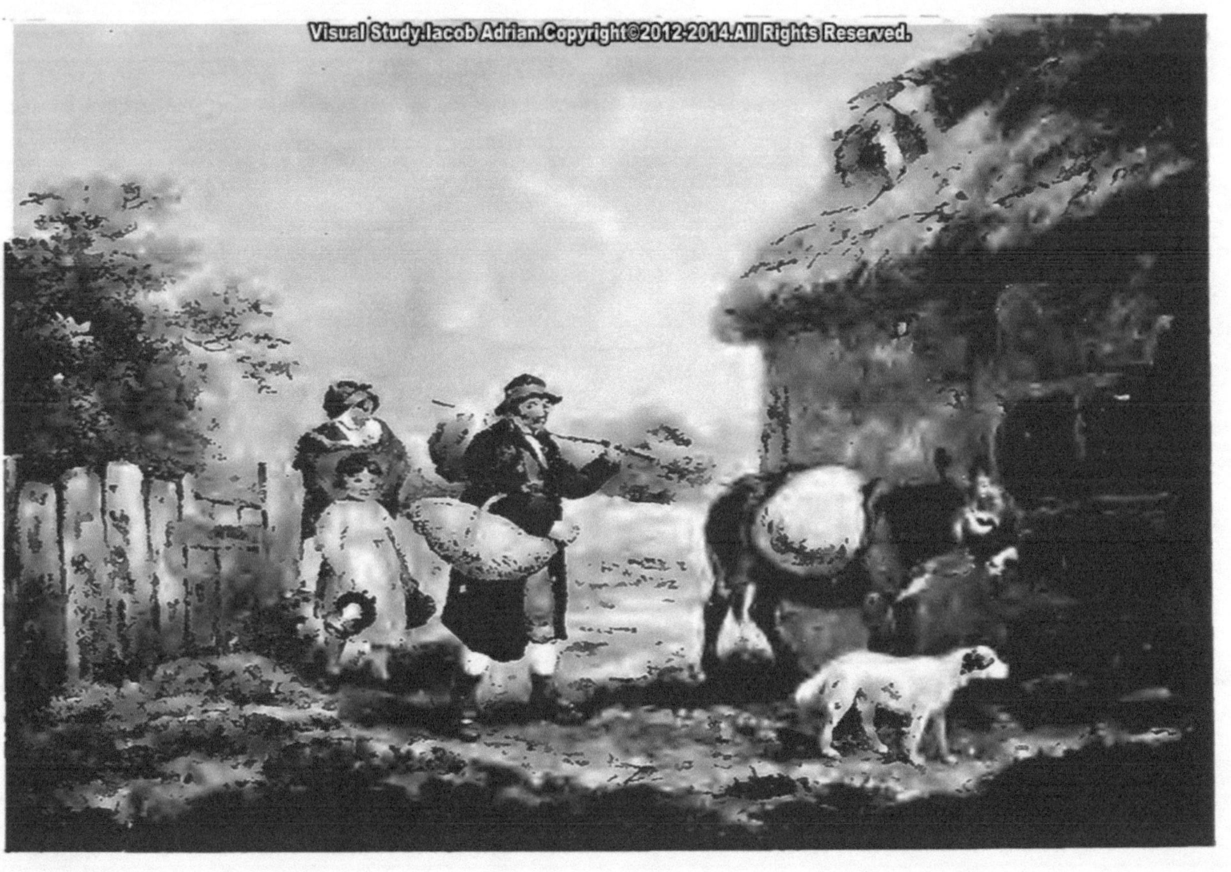

PEASANTS TRAVELLING REISENDE BAUERN PAYSANS VOYAGEANT

(Mrs. F. Abbiss Phillips, Stoke d'Abernon)

H. Hyatt, Photo.

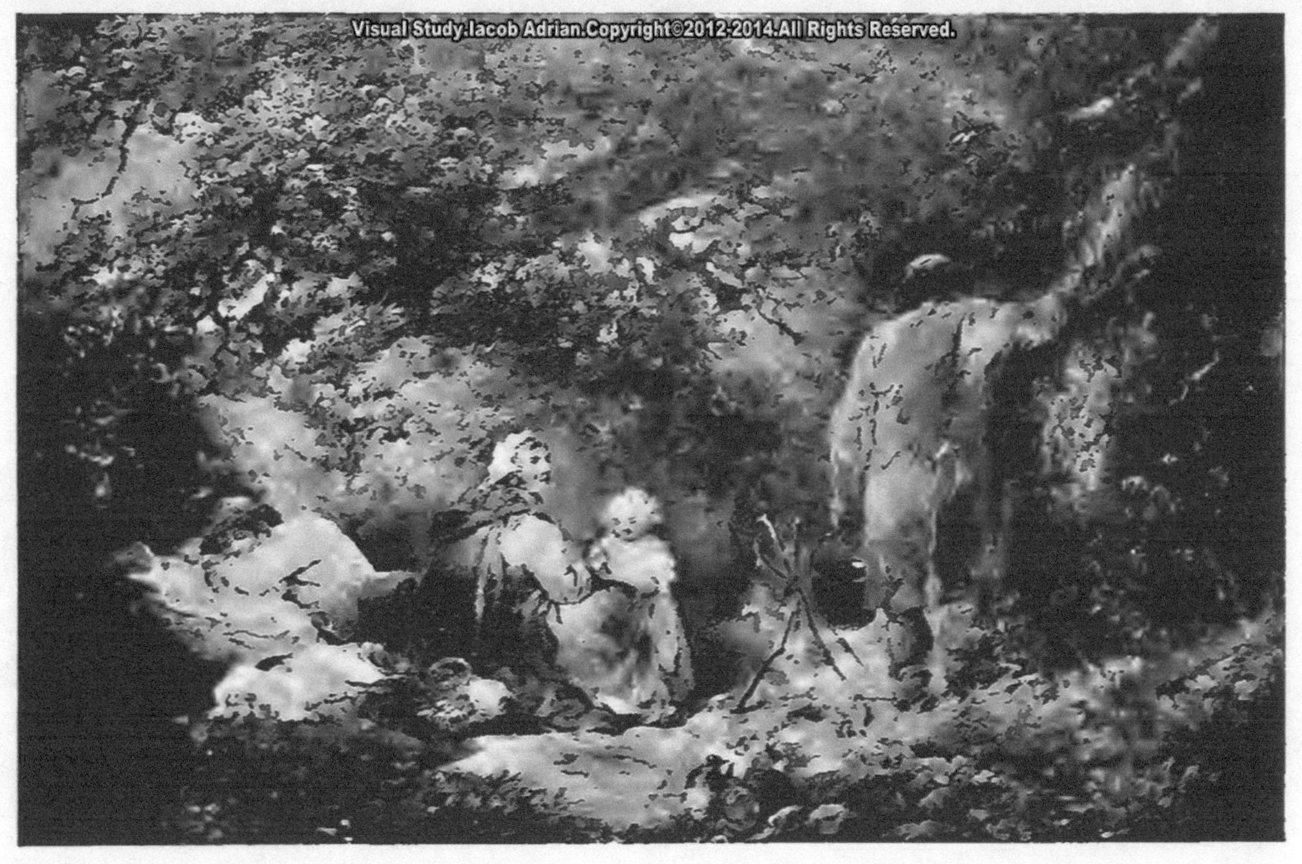

A GIPSY ENCAMPMENT EIN ZIGEUNERLAGER UN CAMPEMENT D'ÉGYPTIENS

(Sir Walter Gilbey, Bart., Elsenham Hall)

J. Caswall Smith, Photo.

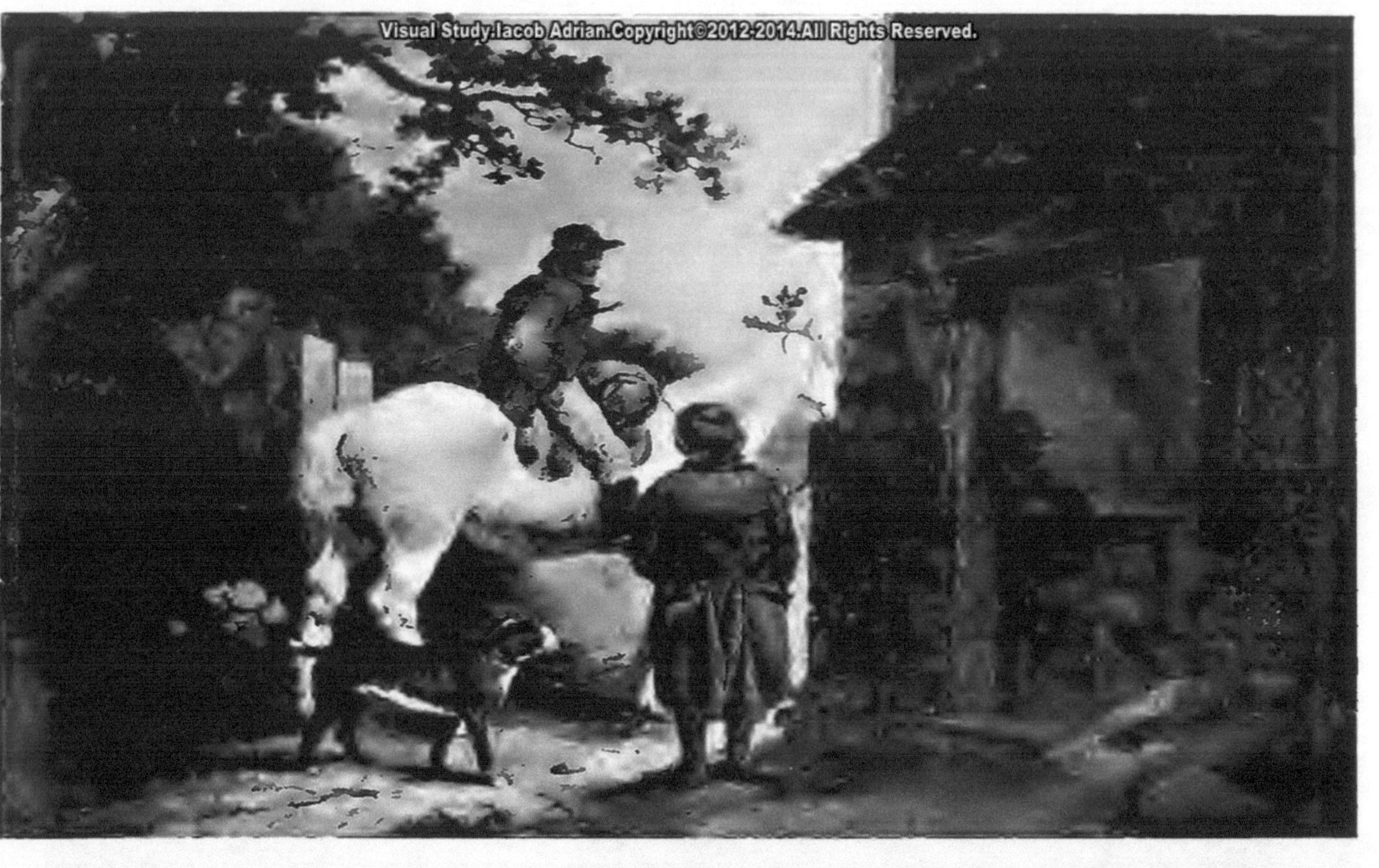

THE TURNPIKE GATE DAS ZOLLTOR LA BARRIÈRE DE PÉAGE

(Mr. John Fleming, London)

J. Caswall Smith, Photo.

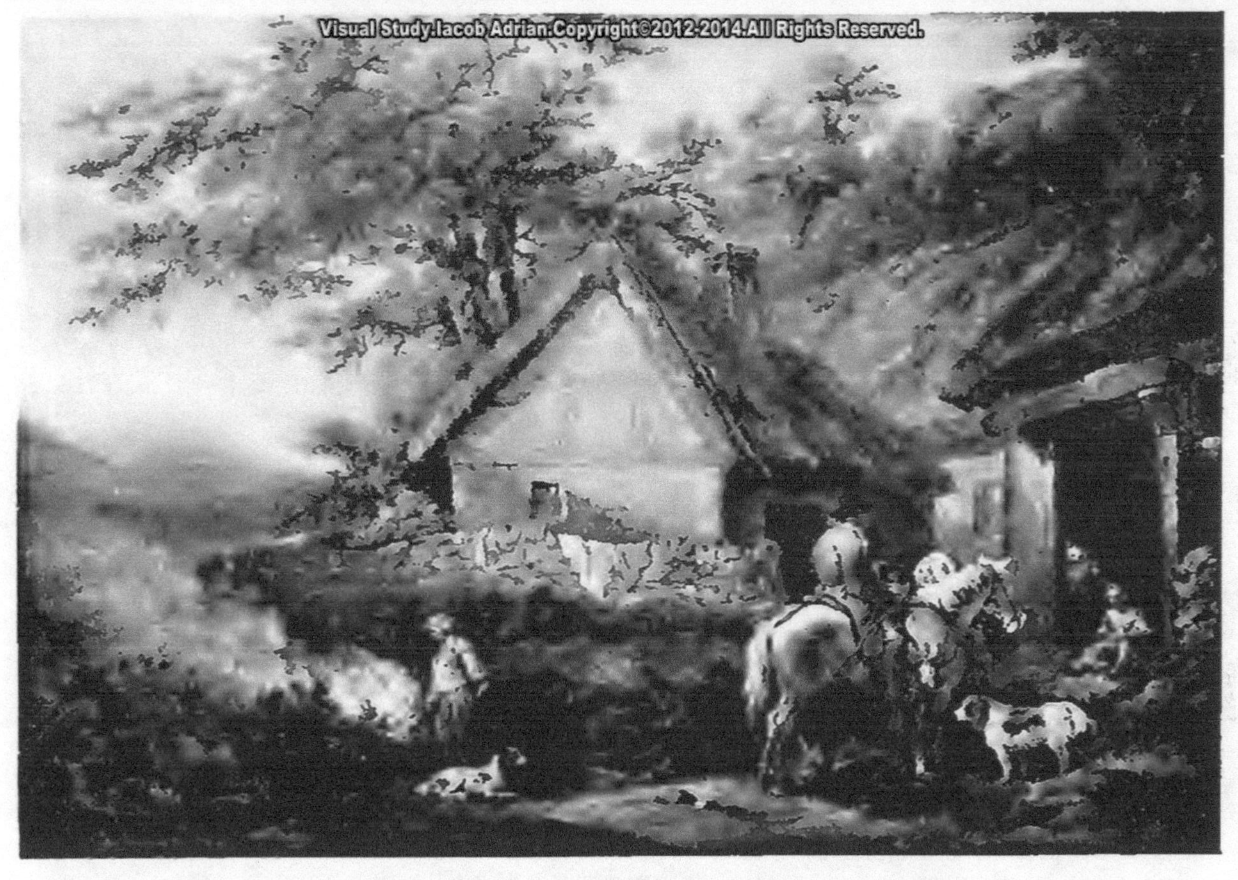

DOOR OF A VILLAGE INN PORTE D'UNE AUBERGE DE VILLAGE

TÜR EINER DORFSCHENKE

(National Gallery, London) *W. A. Mansell & Co., Photo.*

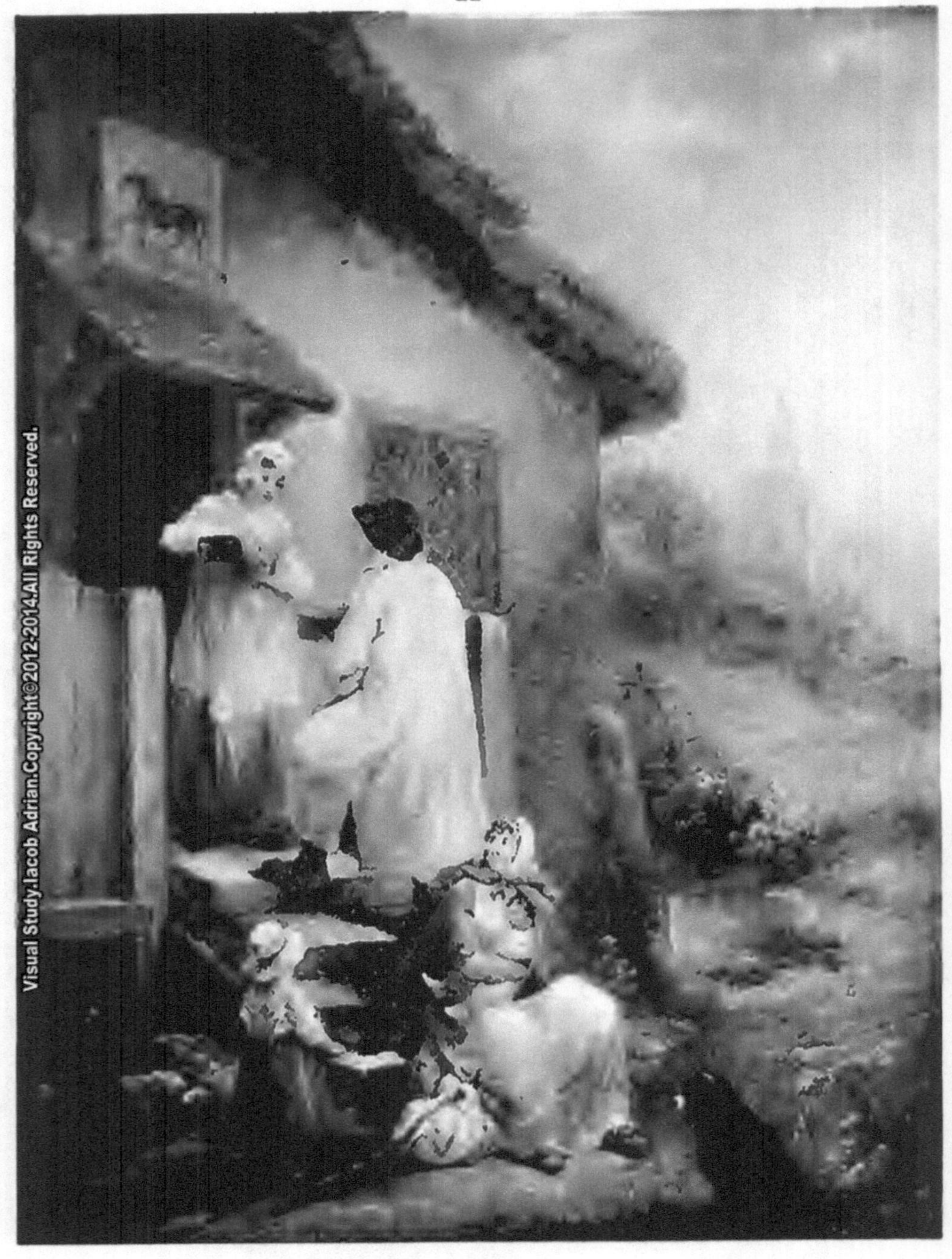

THE DRAM DER SCHLUCK LA GOUTTE

(*Sir Walter Gilbey, Bart., Elsenham Hall*)

J. Caswall Smith, Photo.

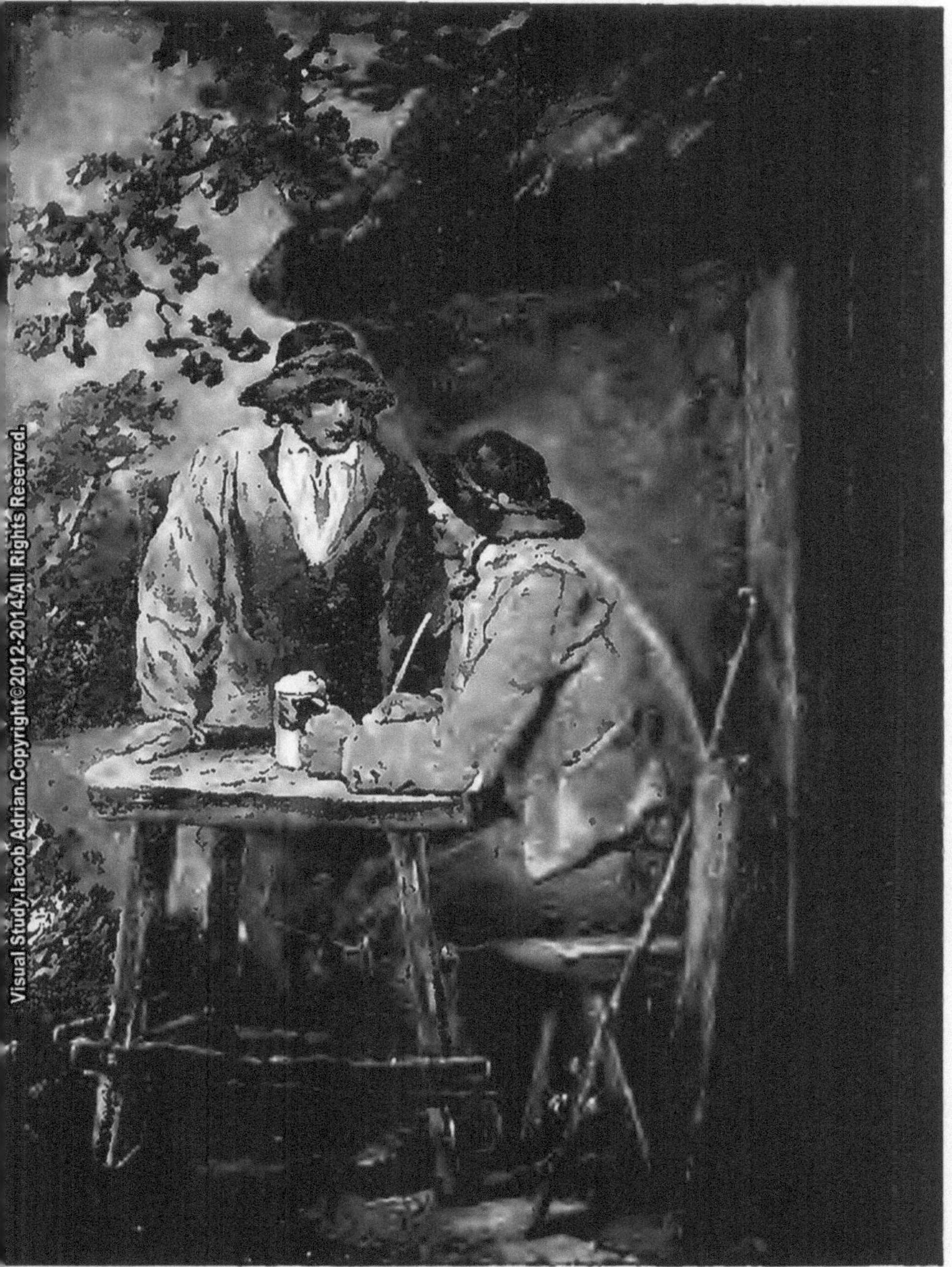

THE ALEHOUSE DOOR   DIE SCHENKENTÜR   LA PORTE D'AUBERGE
(*National Gallery, London*)
J. Caswall Smith, Photo.

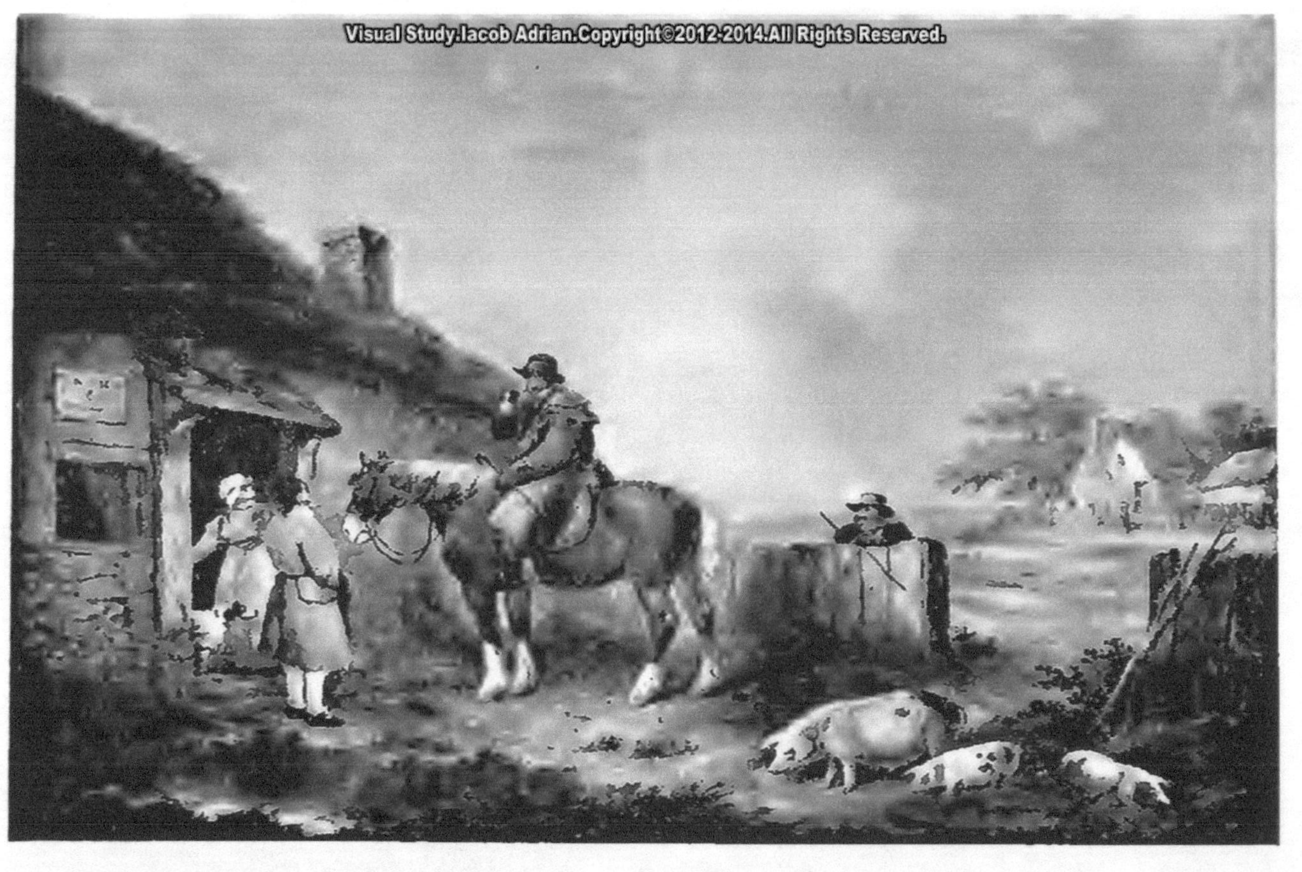

THE RED LION INN — L'AUBERGE DU LION ROUGE

DIE SCHENKE ZUM ROTEN LÖWEN

(Mrs. F. Abbiss Phillips, Stoke d'Abernon) *H. Hyatt, Photo.*

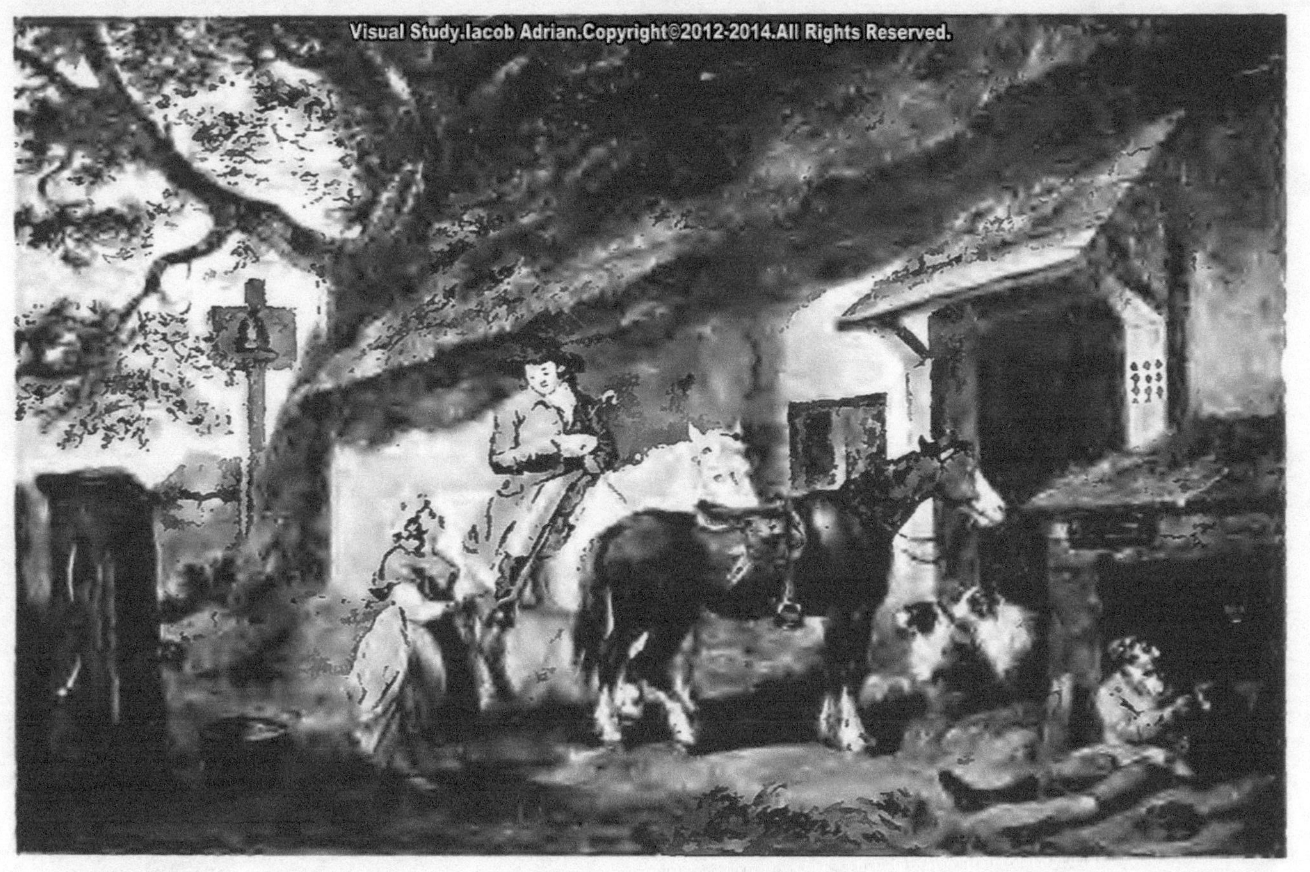

THE HALT — DIE RAST — LA HALTE

(*Louvre, Paris*)

H. Hyatt, Photo.

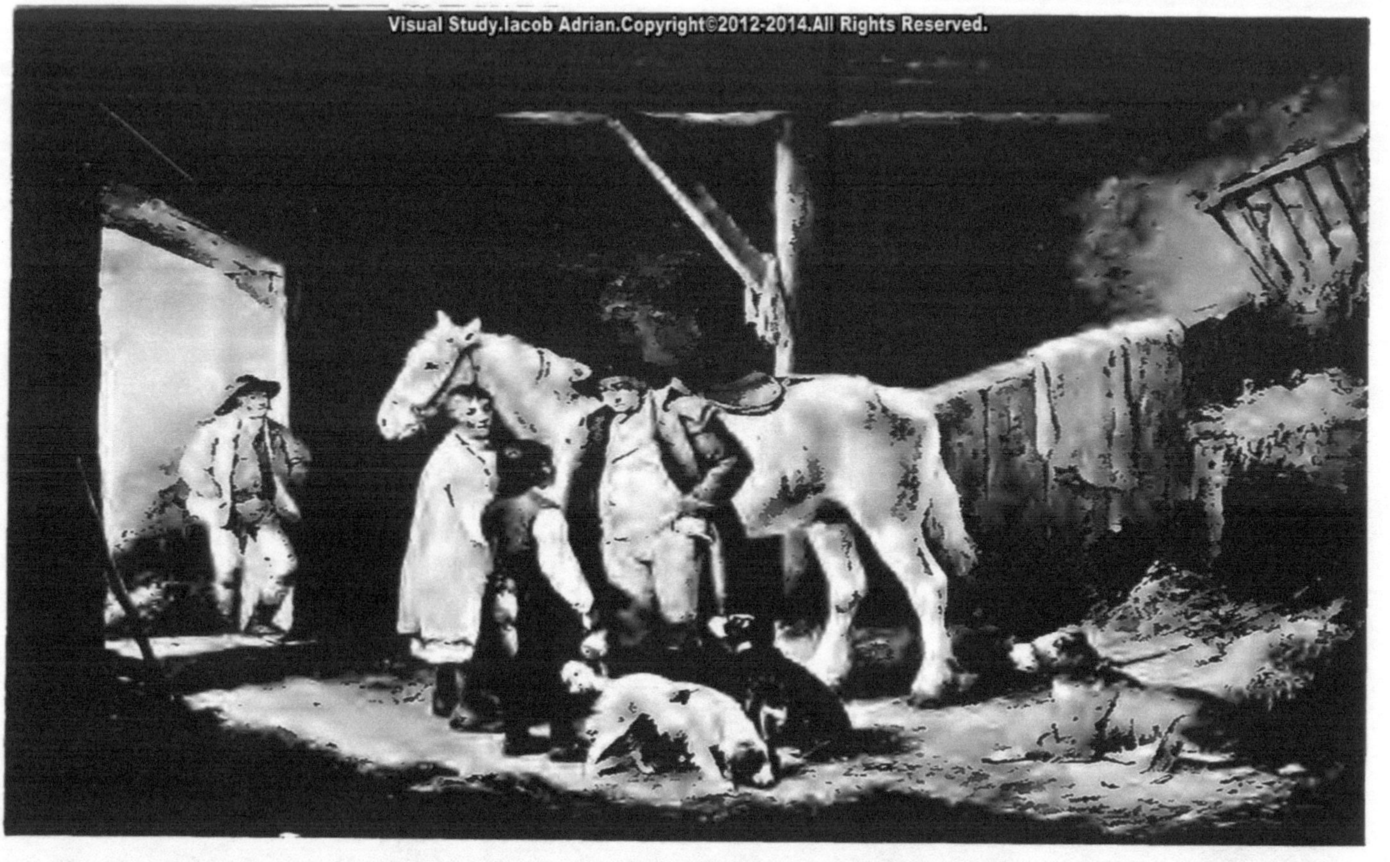

THE RECKONING DIE RECHNUNG L'ÉCOT

(Victoria and Albert Museum, South Kensington)

W. A. Mansell & Co., Photo.

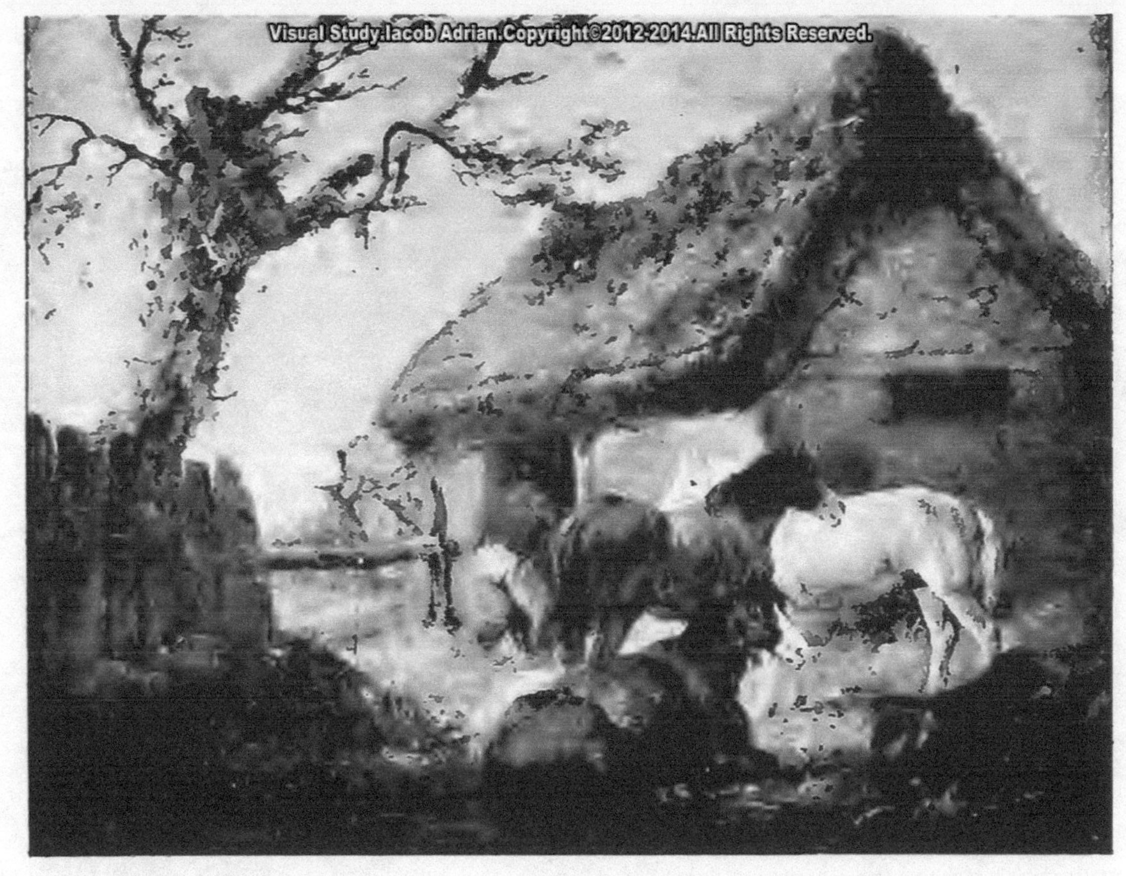

THE STABLE-YARD DER STALLHOF COUR D'ÉCURIE

(Mrs. F. Abbiss Phillips, Stoke d'Abernon)

H. Hyatt, Photo.

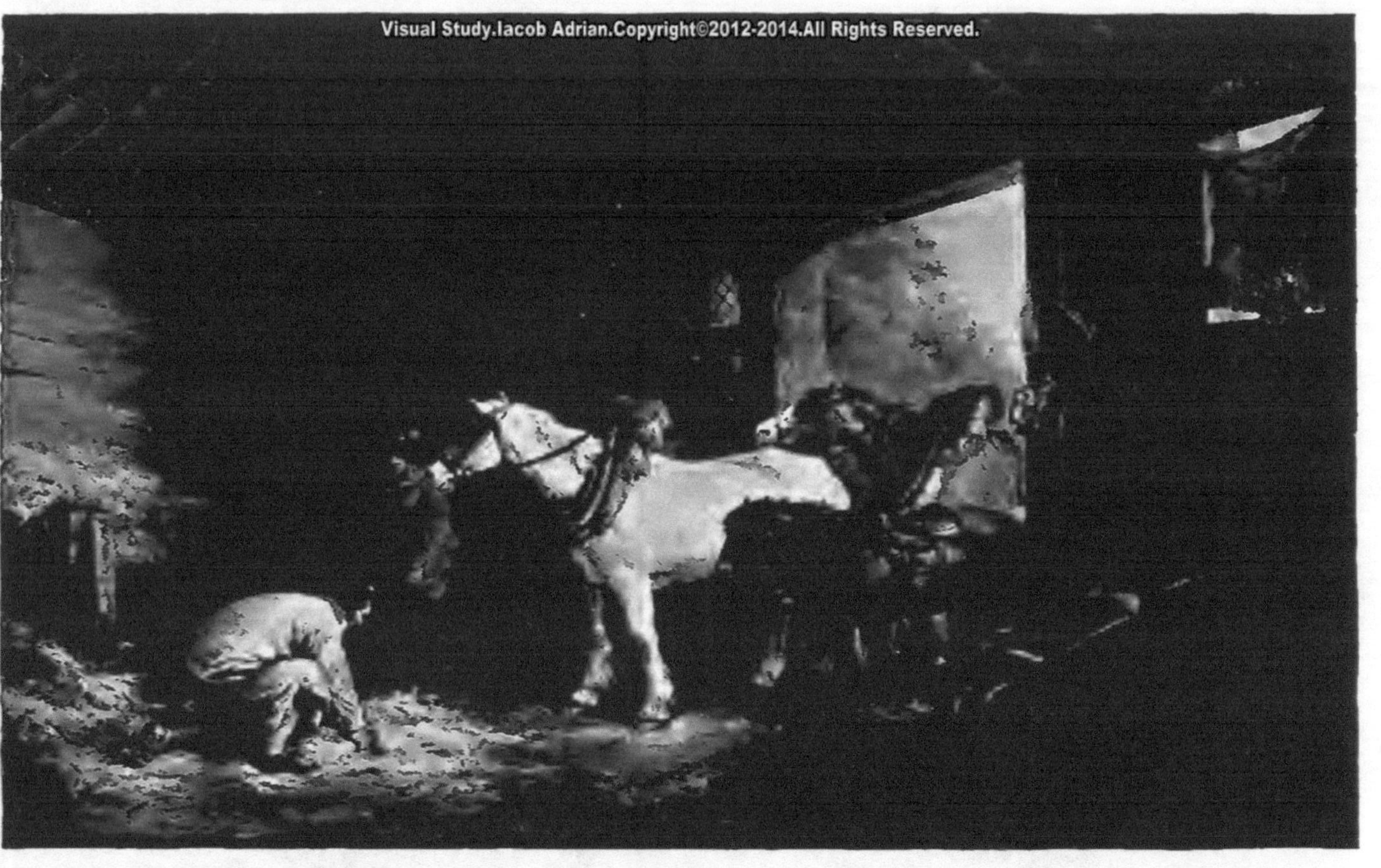

The Inside of a Stable   Das Innere eines Stalles   L'Intérieur d'une Écurie

(*National Gallery, London*)

F. Hanfstaengl, Photo.

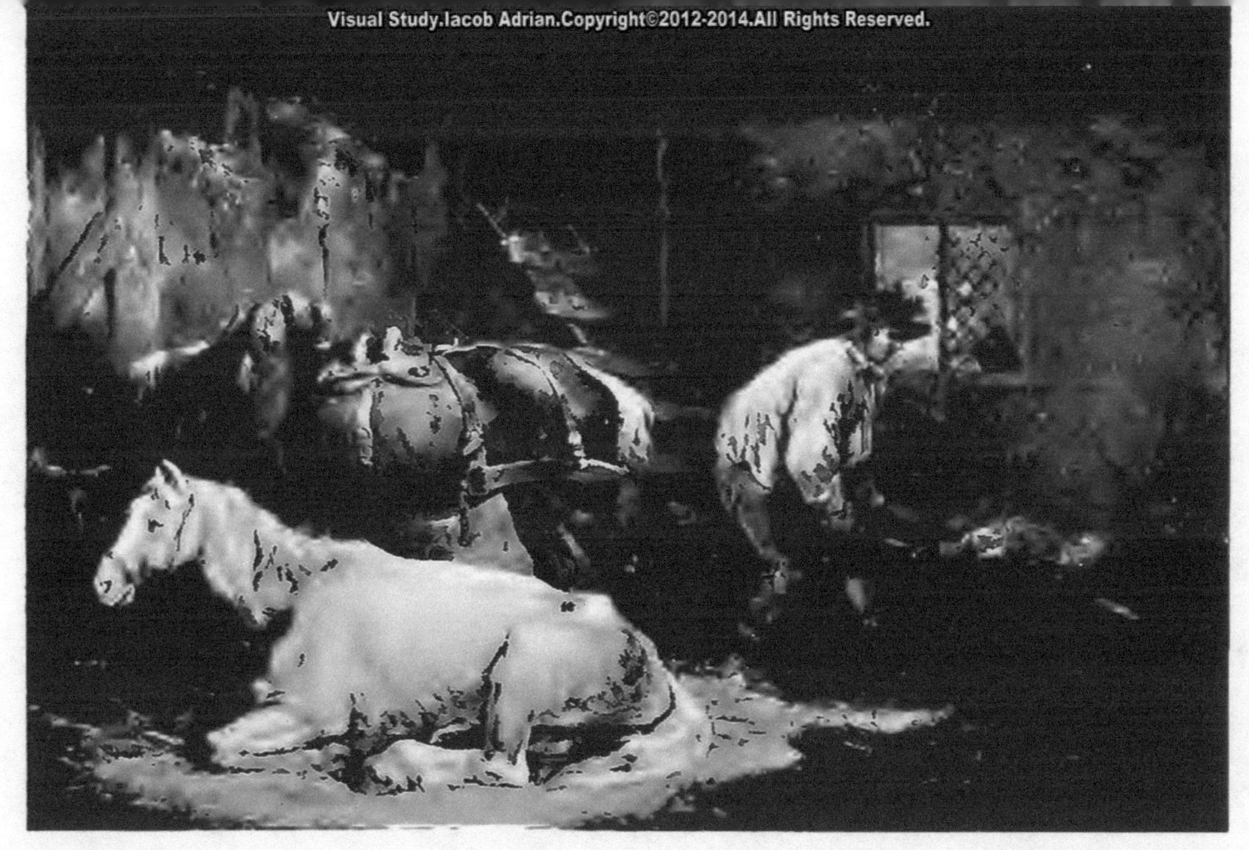

Horses in a Stable   Chevaux dans une Écurie

Pferde in einem Stall

(Victoria and Albert Museum, South Kensington)   *J. Caswall Smith, Photo.*

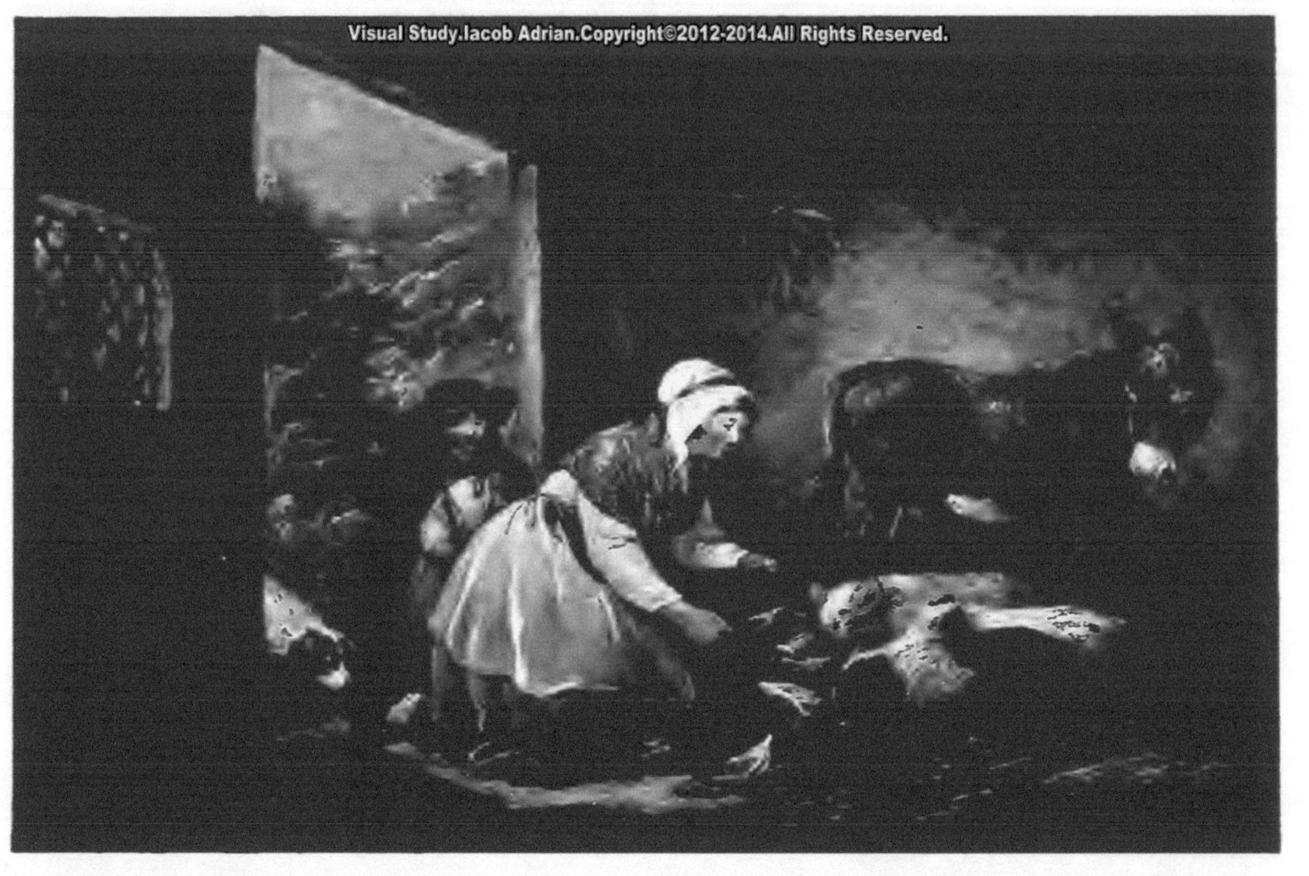

WOMAN FEEDING PIGS FEMME DONNANT A MANGER AUX COCHONS

WEIB SCHWEINE FÜTTERND

(Mrs. F. Abbiss Phillips, Stoke d'Abernon) *H. Hyatt, Photo.*

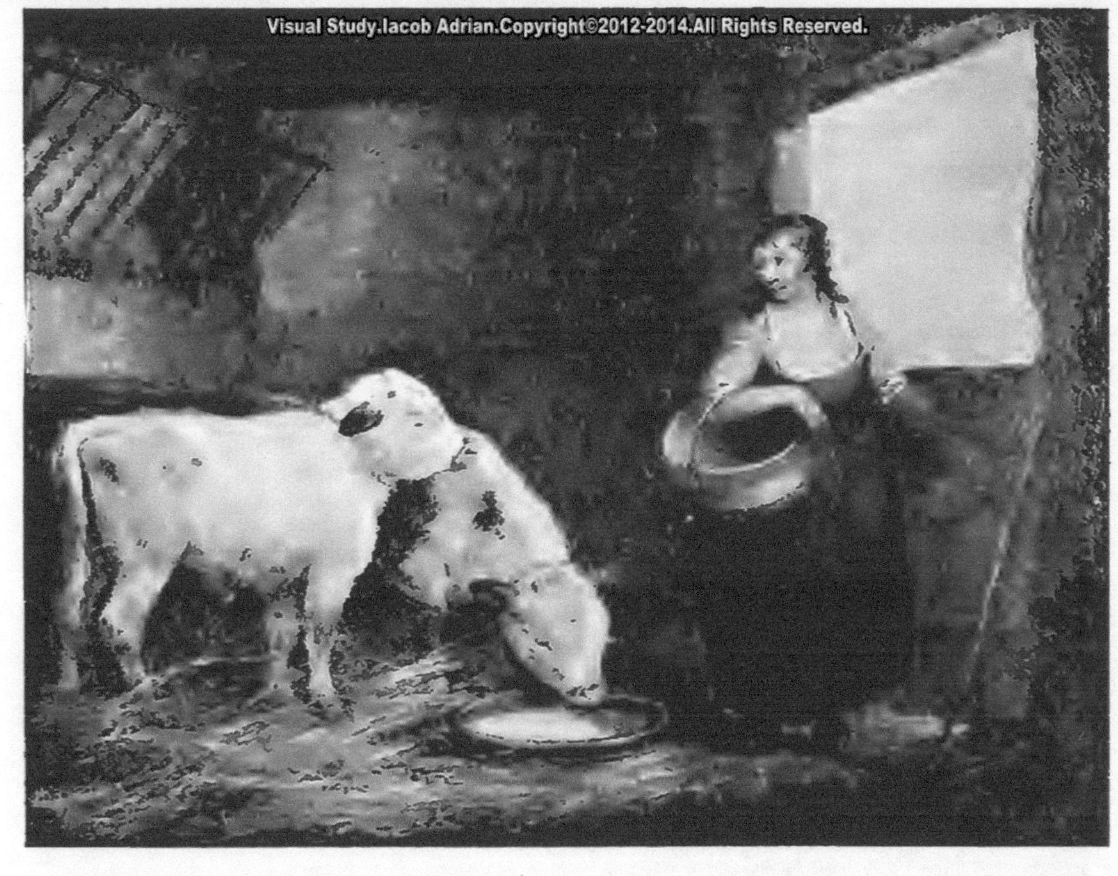

Feeding the Calves — Donnant a manger aux Veaux

Fütterung der Kälber

(Mrs. F. Abbiss Phillips, Stoke d'Abernon) *H. Hyatt, Photo.*

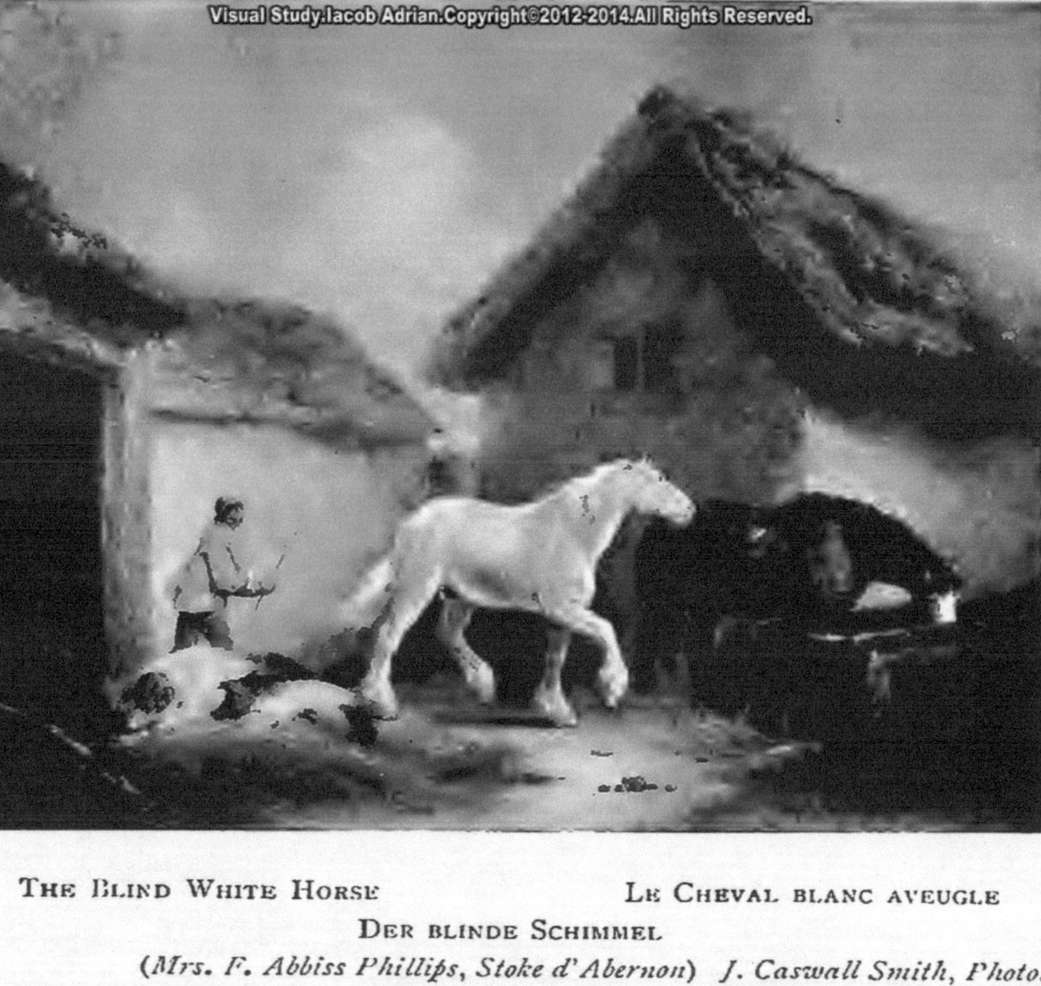

THE BLIND WHITE HORSE   LE CHEVAL BLANC AVEUGLE

DER BLINDE SCHIMMEL

(*Mrs. F. Abbiss Phillips, Stoke d'Abernon*) *J. Caswall Smith, Photo.*

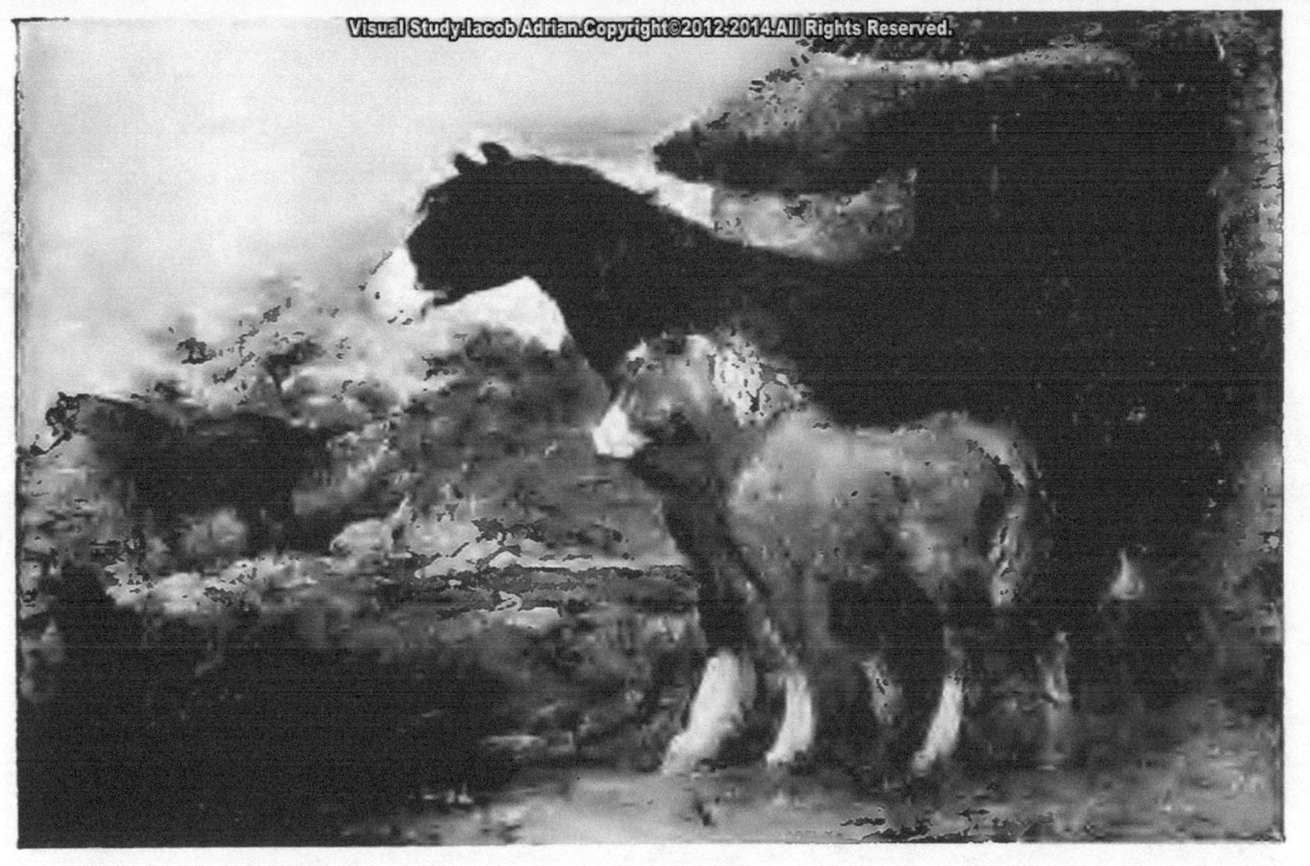

MARE AND FOAL STUTE UND FÜLLEN JUMENT ET POULAIN

(Mr. John Fleming, London)

J. Caswall Smith, Photo.

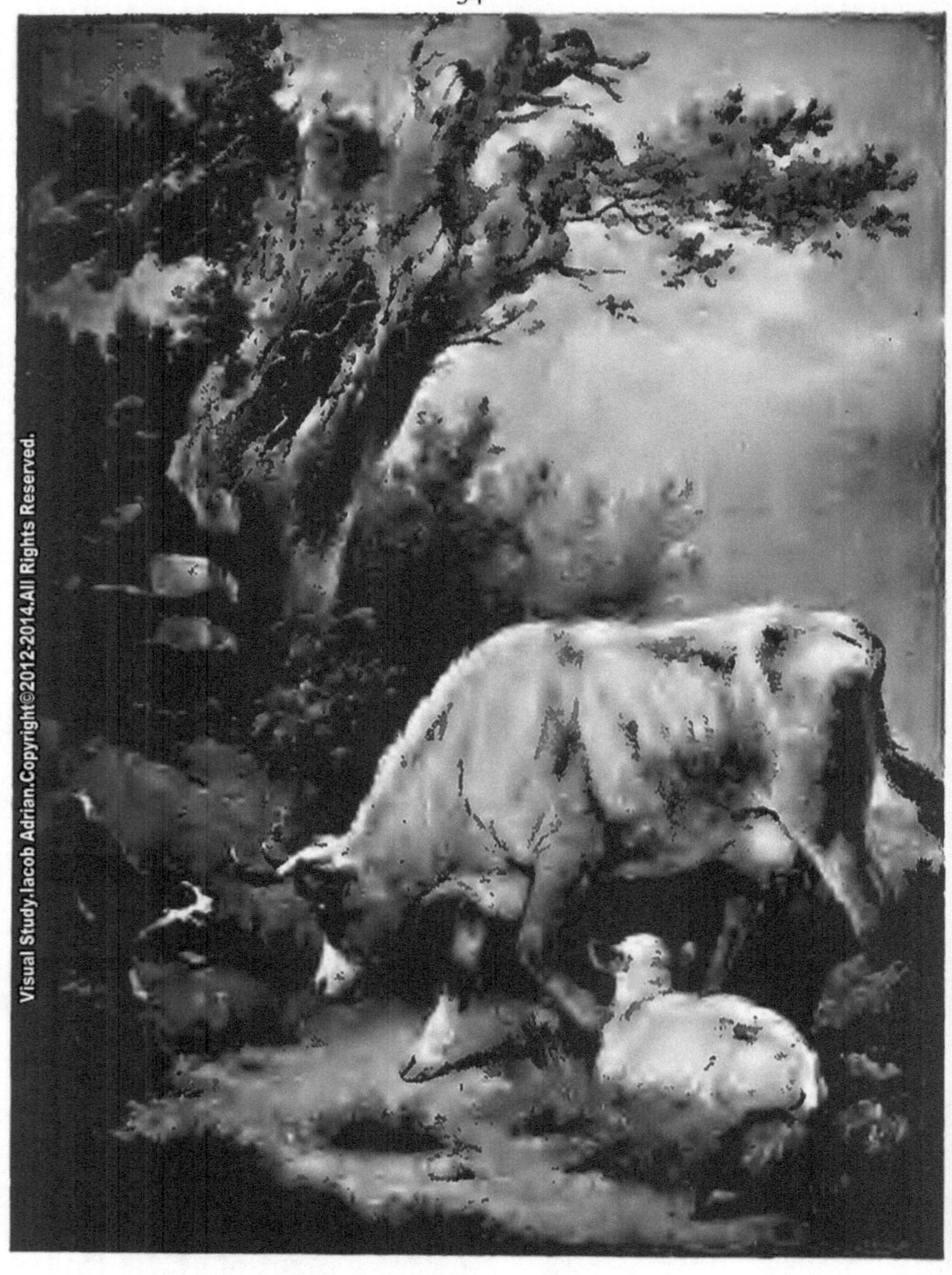

COW AND DOG KUH UND HUND VACHE ET CHIEN

(Mrs. F. Abbiss Phillips, Stoke d'Abernon)

H. Hyatt, Photo.

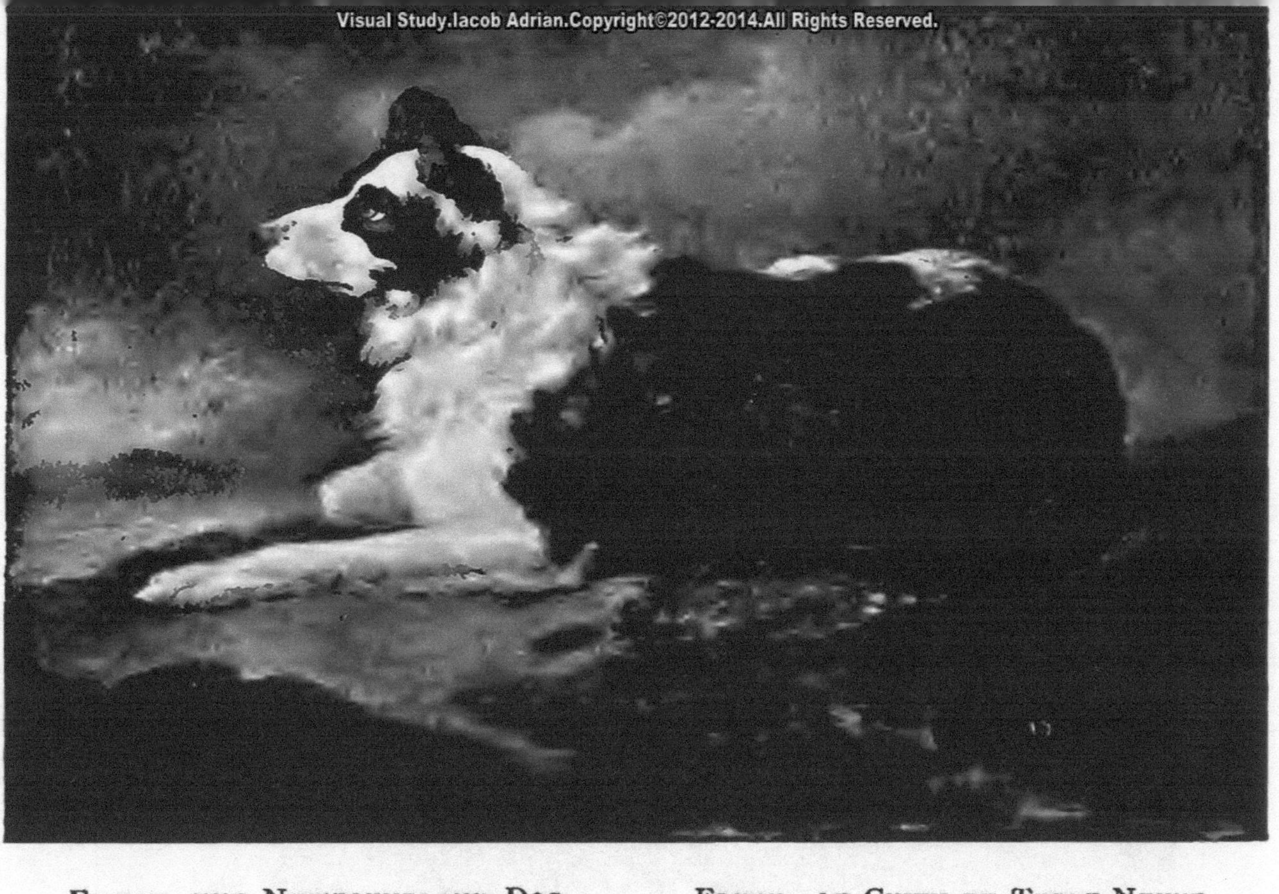

FRIEND, THE NEWFOUNDLAND DOG FRIEND, LE CHIEN DE TERRE-NEUVE
FRIEND, DER NEUFUNDLÄNDER
(Mrs. F. Abbiss Phillips, Stoke d'Abernon) *H. Hyatt, Photo.*

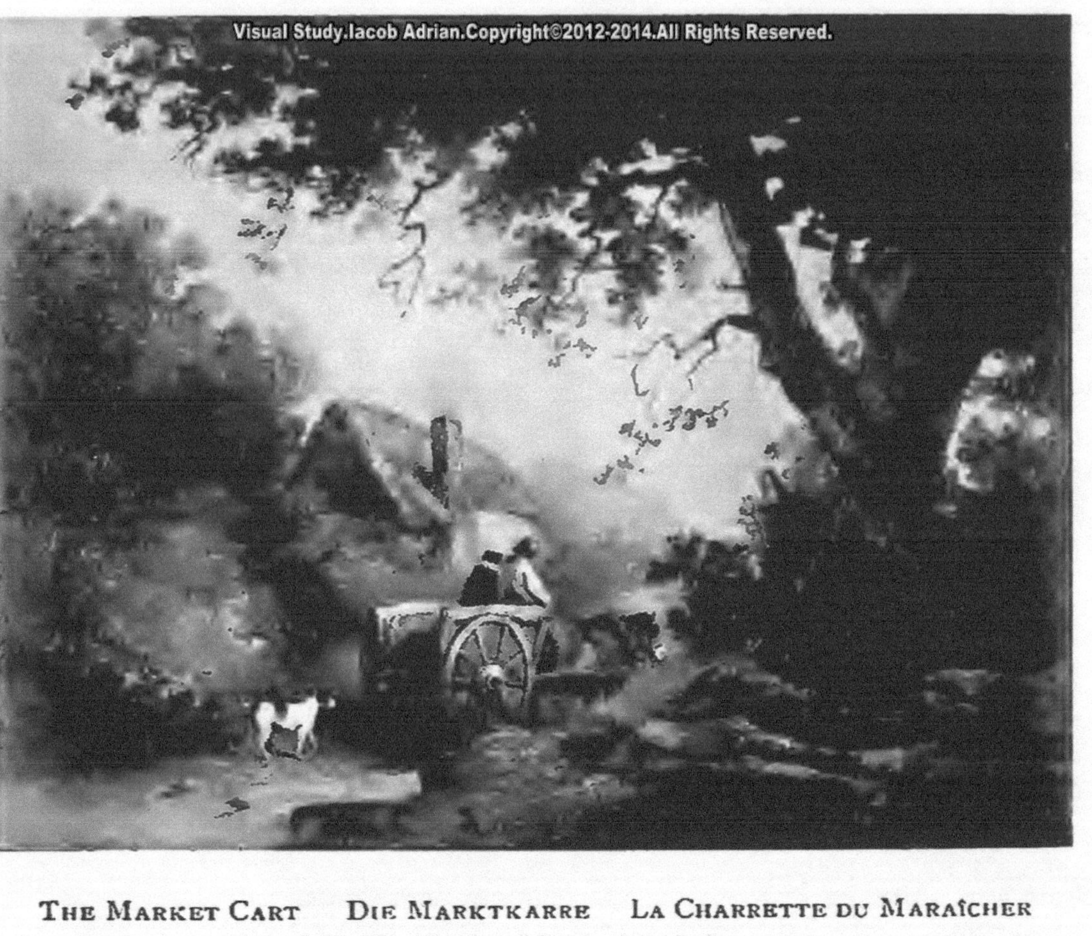

THE MARKET CART DIE MARKTKARRE LA CHARRETTE DU MARAÎCHER

(Mr. G. Harland-Peck, London)

J. Caswall Smith, Photo.

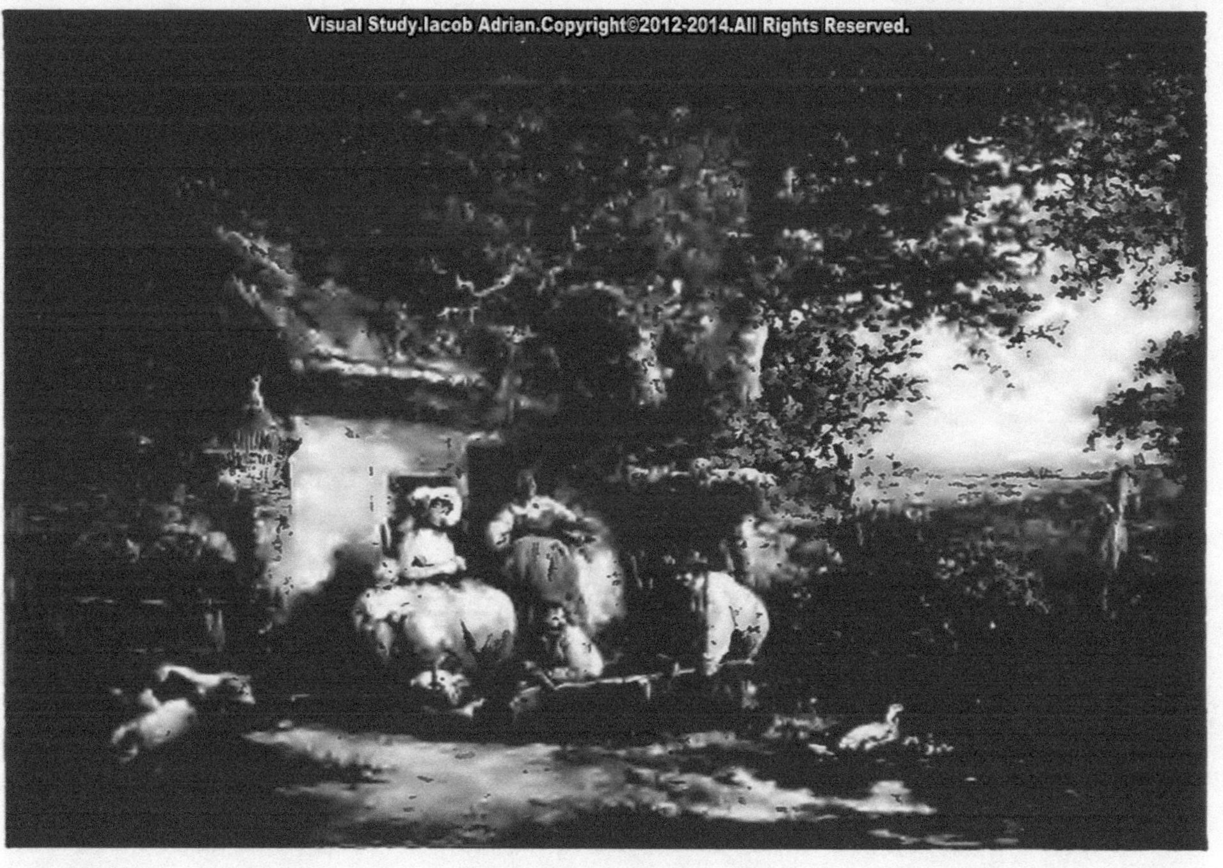

THE HAPPY COTTAGERS   DIE GLÜCKLICHE HÜTTLER   LES PAYSANS HEUREUX

(Mr. Frank T. Sabin, London)

Henry Dixon & Son, Photo.

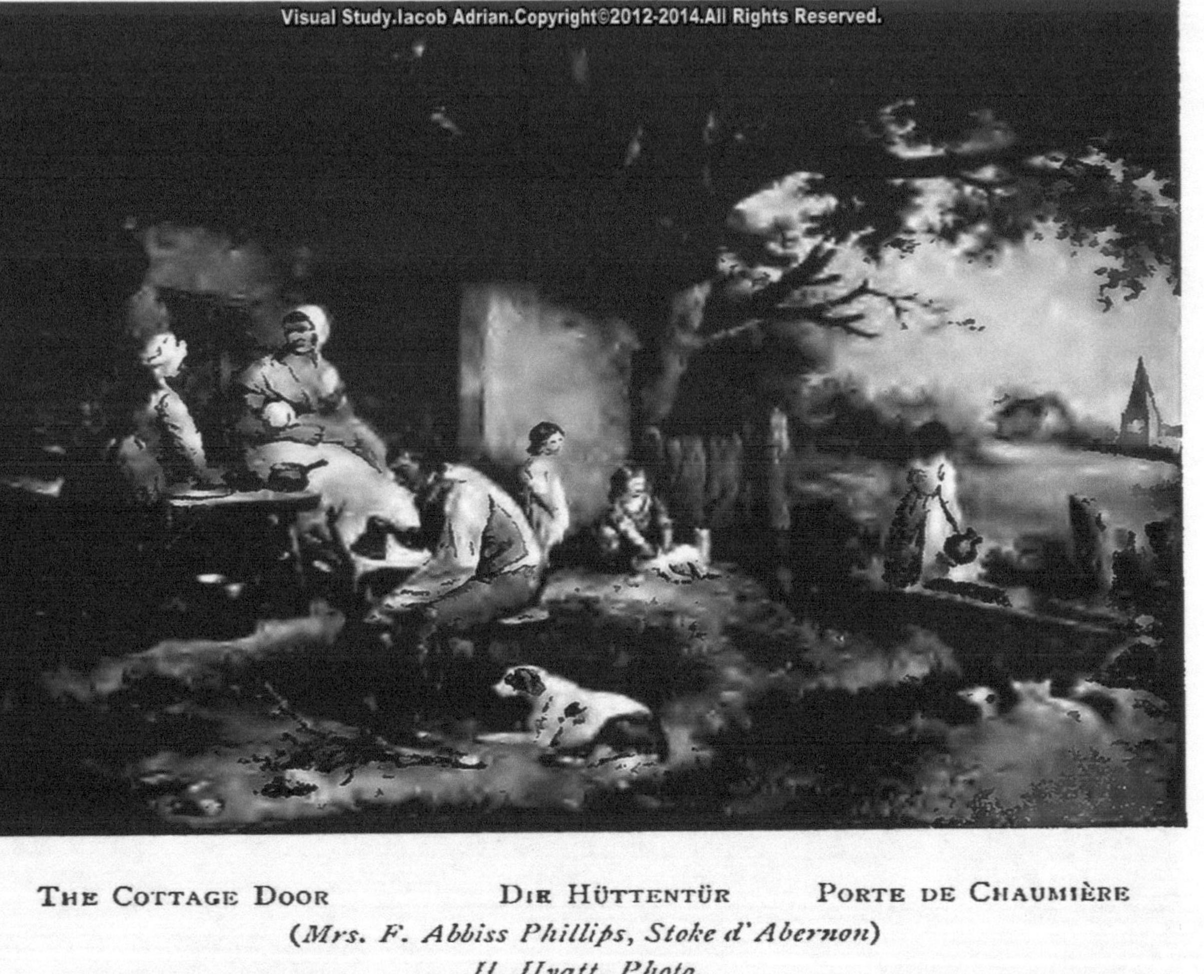

THE COTTAGE DOOR DIE HÜTTENTÜR PORTE DE CHAUMIÈRE

(Mrs. F. Abbiss Phillips, Stoke d'Abernon)

H. Hyatt, Photo.

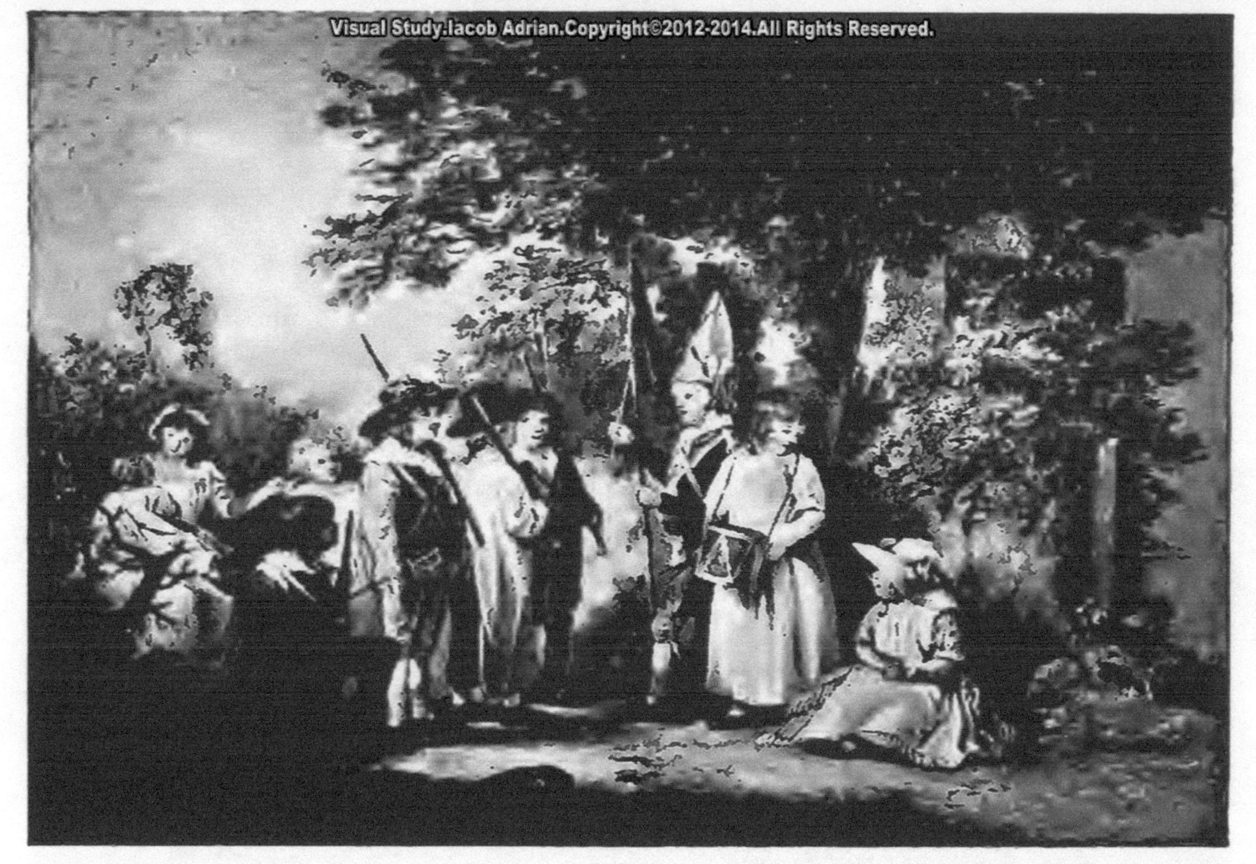

Children playing at Soldiers   Enfants jouant aux Soldats

Soldatspielende Kinder

(*Lord Glenconner, London*)   *J. Caswall Smith, Photo.*

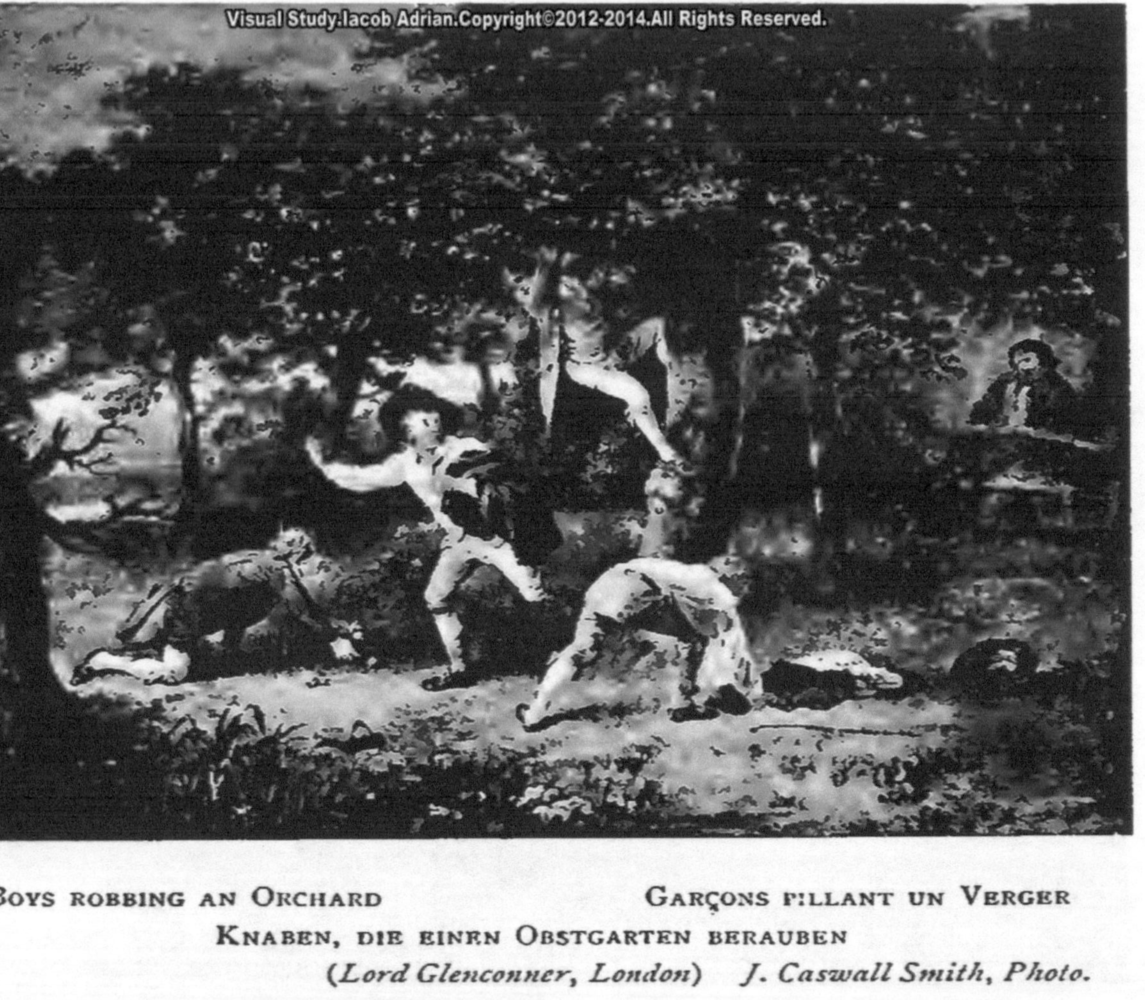

Boys robbing an Orchard　　Garçons pillant un Verger

Knaben, die einen Obstgarten berauben

(Lord Glenconner, London)　*J. Caswall Smith, Photo.*

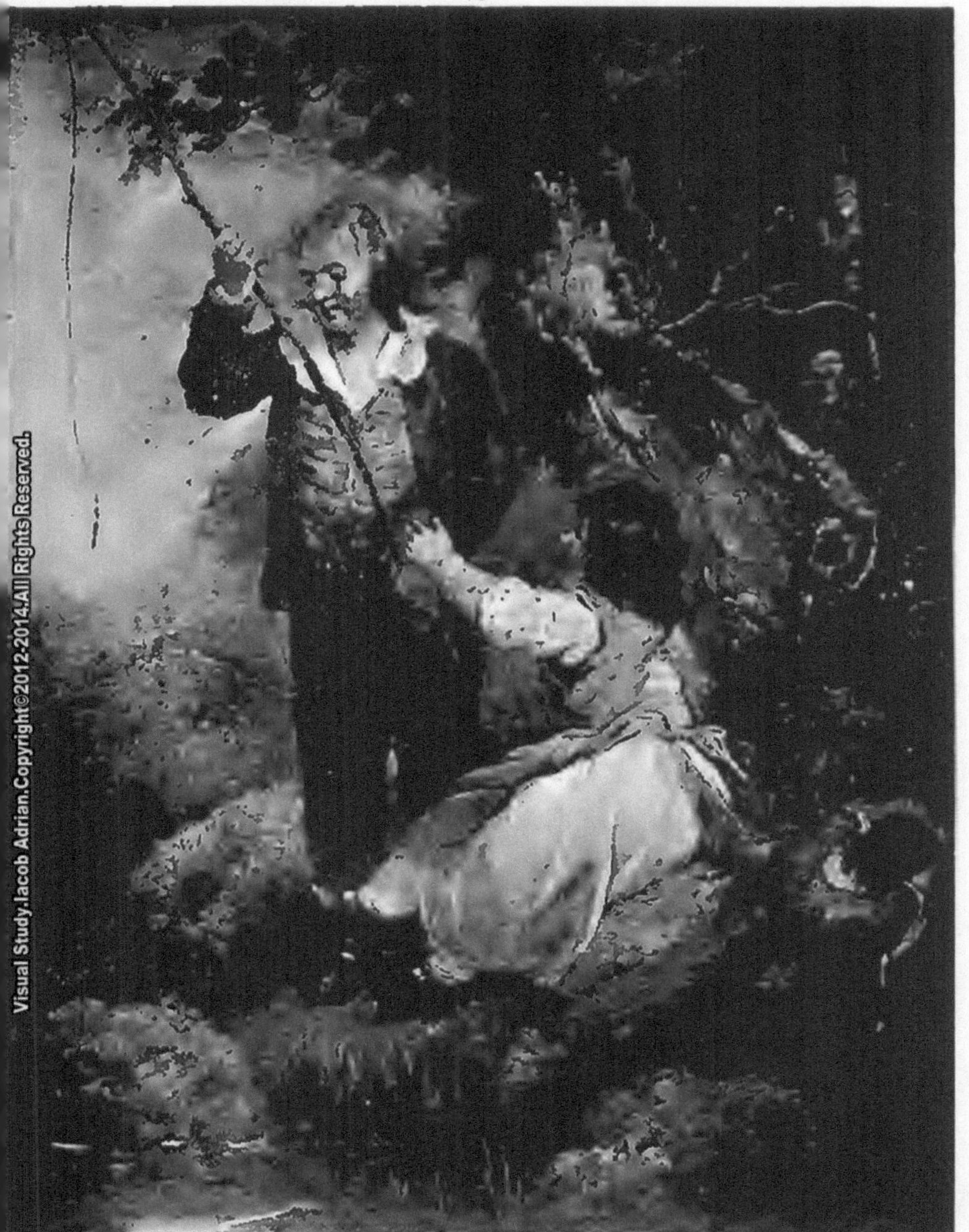

CHILDREN FISHING — ENFANTS PÊCHANT A LA LIGNE

FISCHENDE KINDER

(Mr. G. Harland-Peck, London)

J. Caswall Smith, Photo.

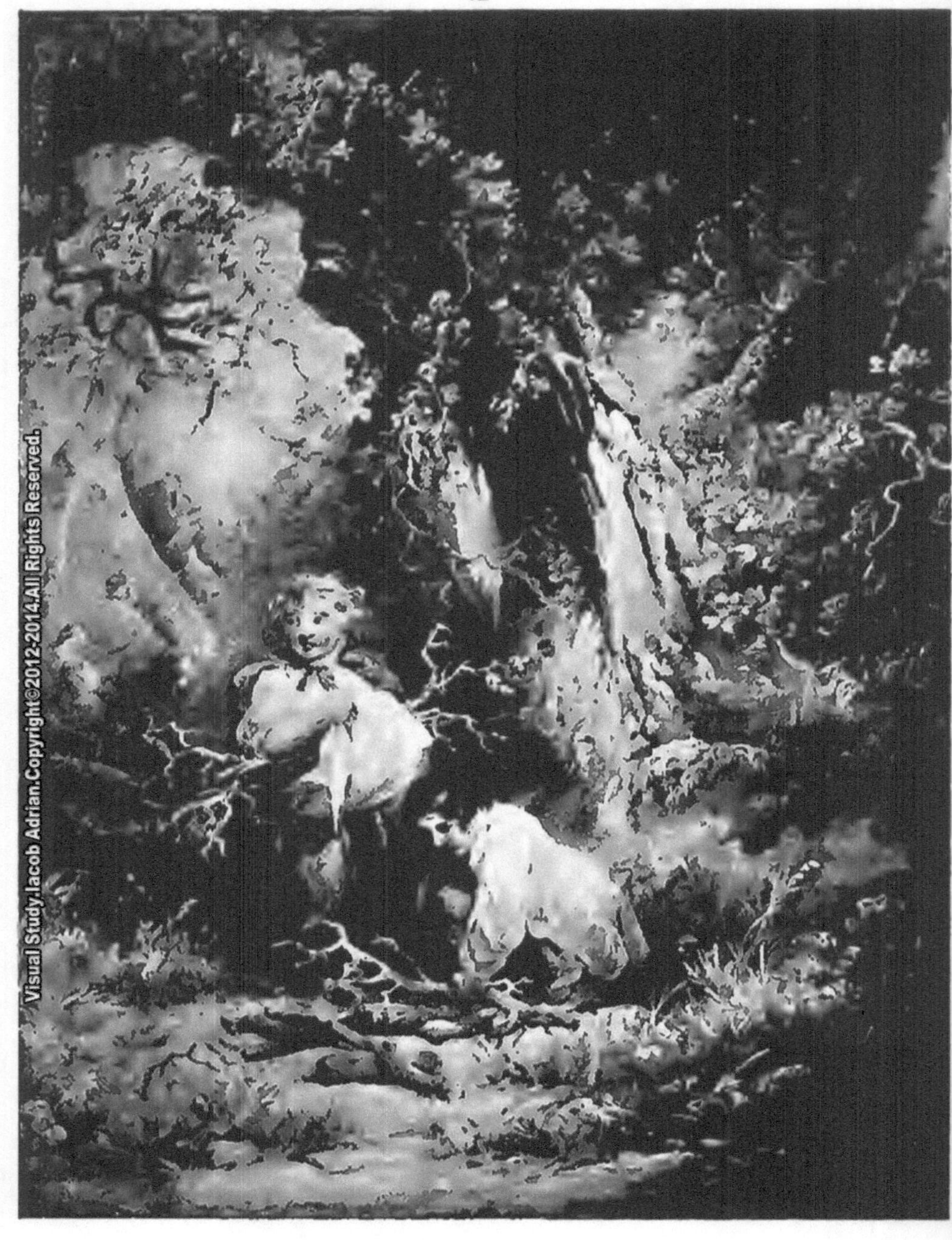

GATHERING STICKS RAMASSANT DU BOIS MORT

HOLZSAMMELN

(*Sir Walter Gilbey, Bart., Elsenham Hall*)

J. Caswall Smith, Photo.

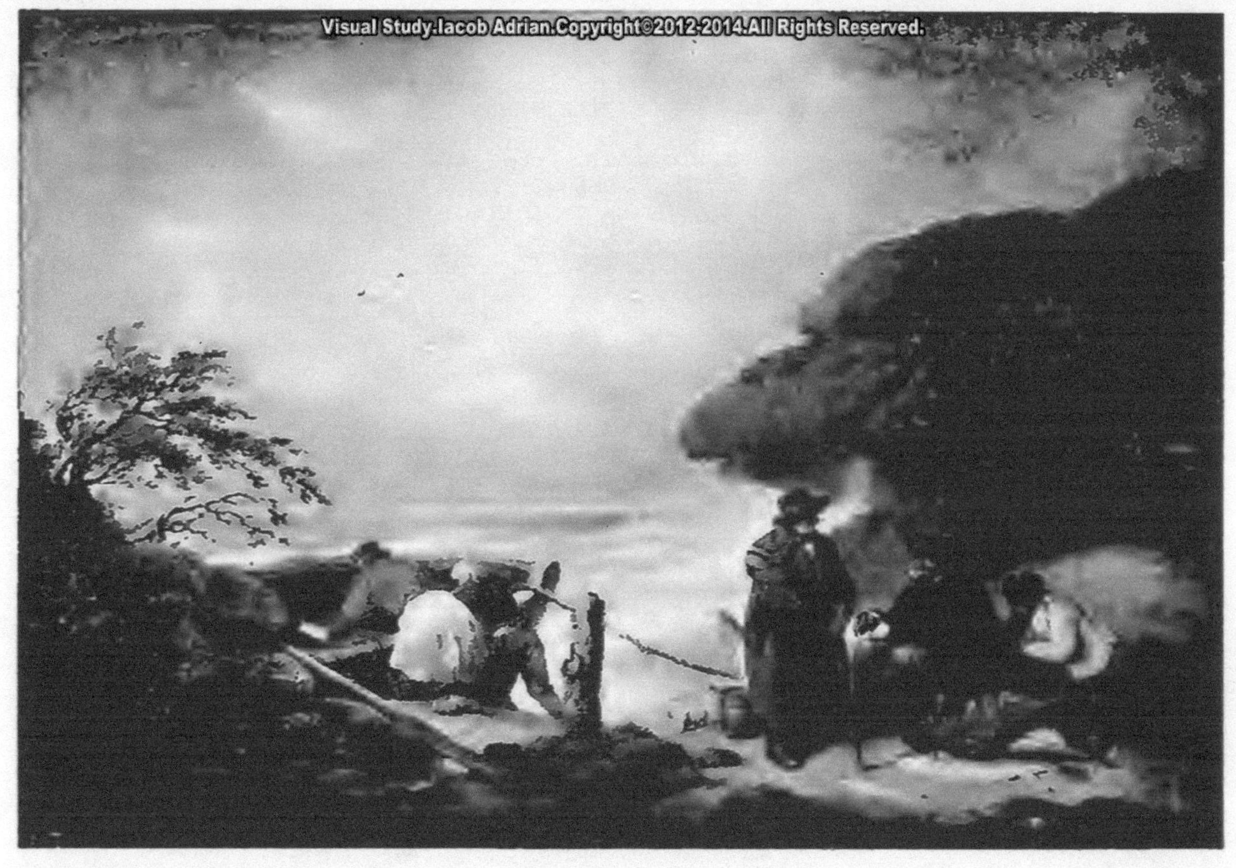

BARGAINING FOR FISH CONCLUANT UN MARCHÉ POUR DU POISSON

ABSCHLUSS EINES FISCHHANDELS

(*Mrs. F. Abbiss Phillips, Stoke d'Abernon*) *H. Hyatt, Photo.*

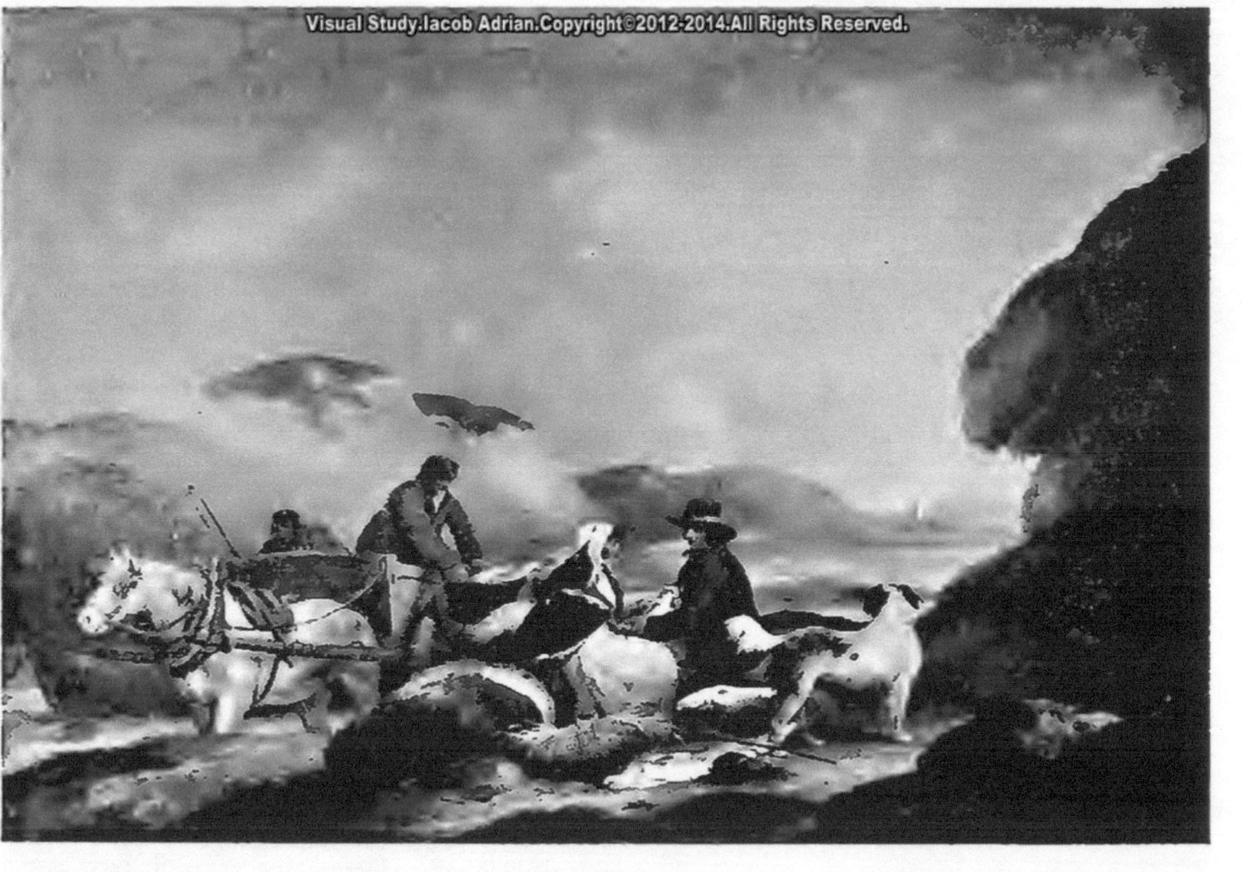

SELLING FISH FISCHVERKAUF VENDANT DU POISSON

(Mrs. F. Abbiss Phillips, Stoke d'Abernon)

H. Hyatt, Photo

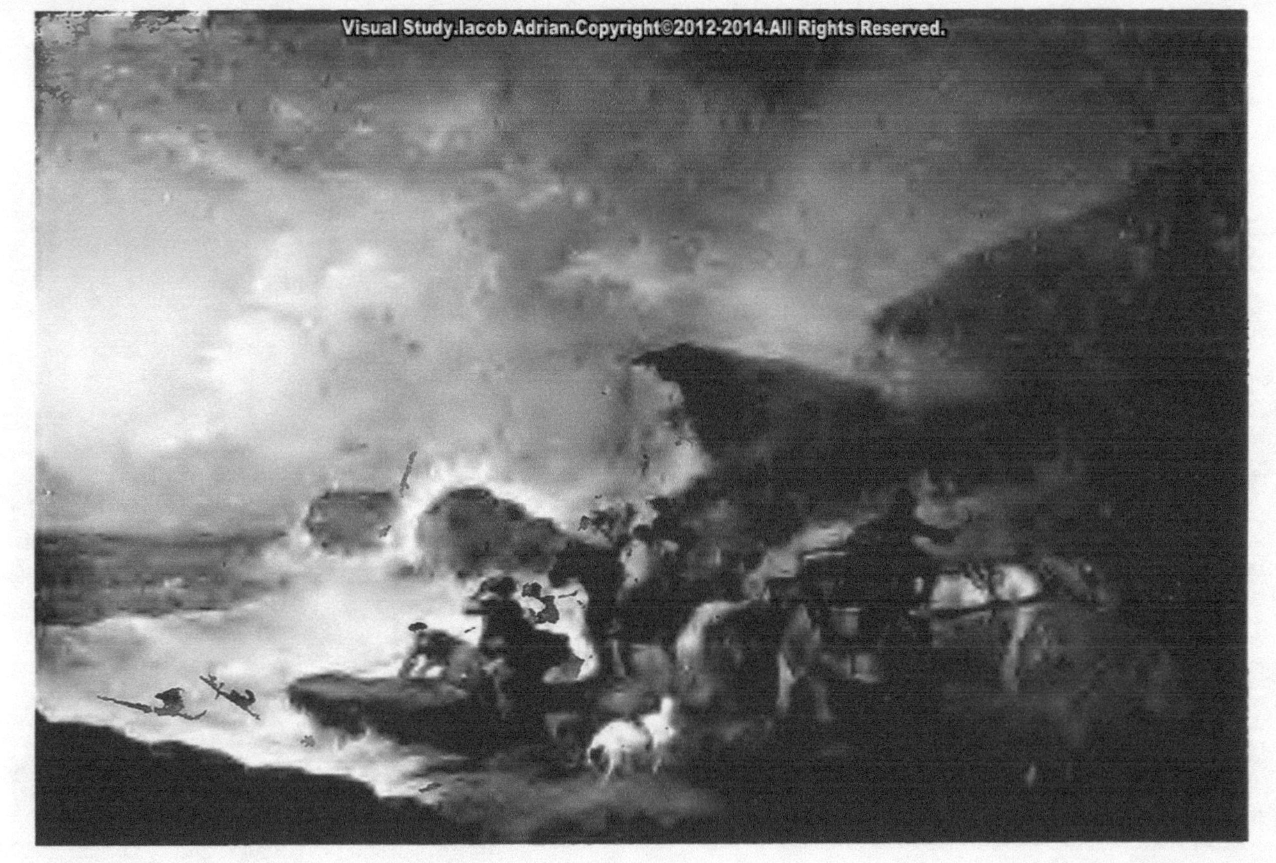

WRECKERS STRANDRÄUBER NAUFRAGEURS

(Sir Walter Gilbey, Bart., Elsenham Hall)

J. Caswall Smith, Photo.

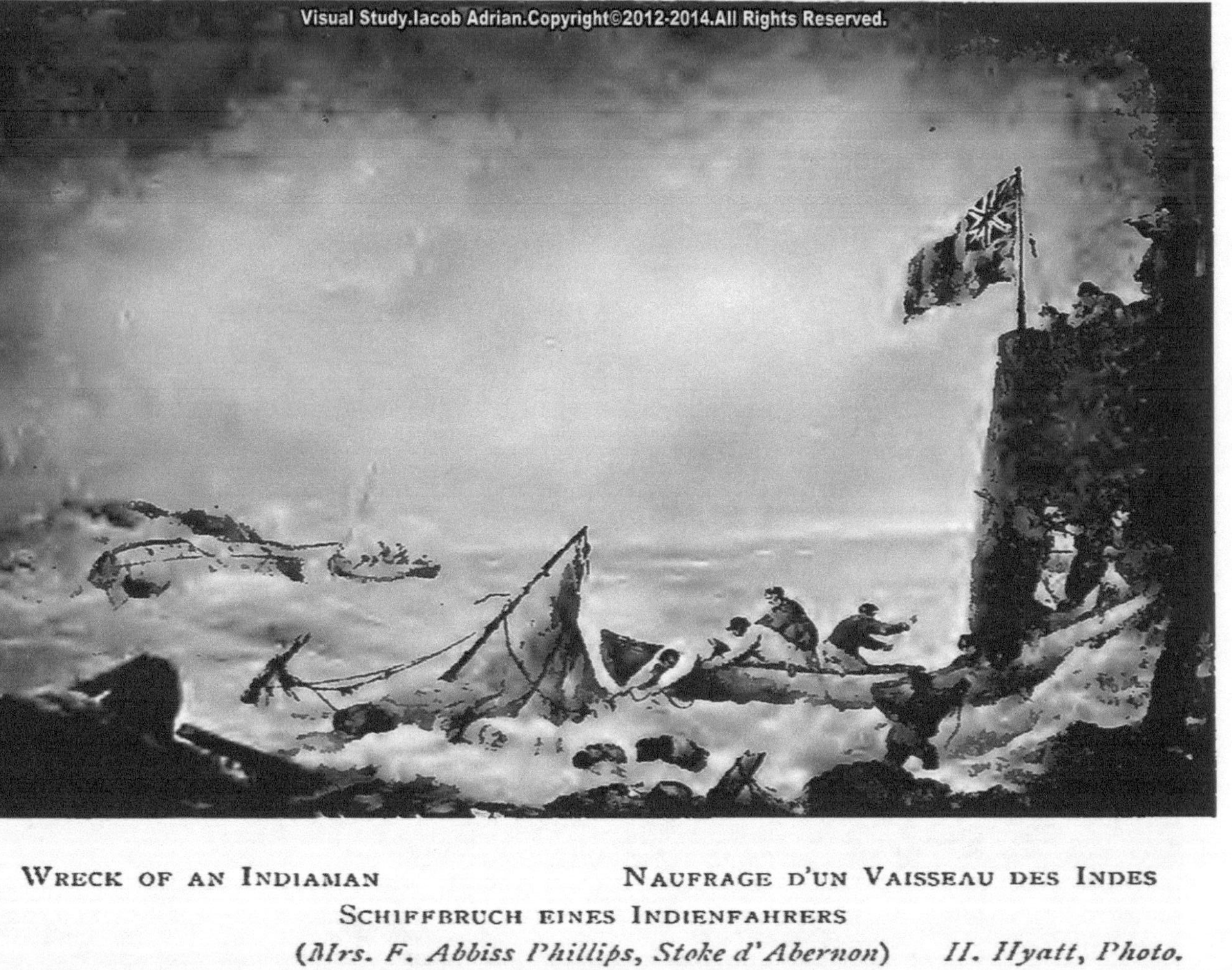

WRECK OF AN INDIAMAN — NAUFRAGE D'UN VAISSEAU DES INDES

SCHIFFBRUCH EINES INDIENFAHRERS

(Mrs. F. Abbiss Phillips, Stoke d'Abernon) — *H. Hyatt, Photo.*

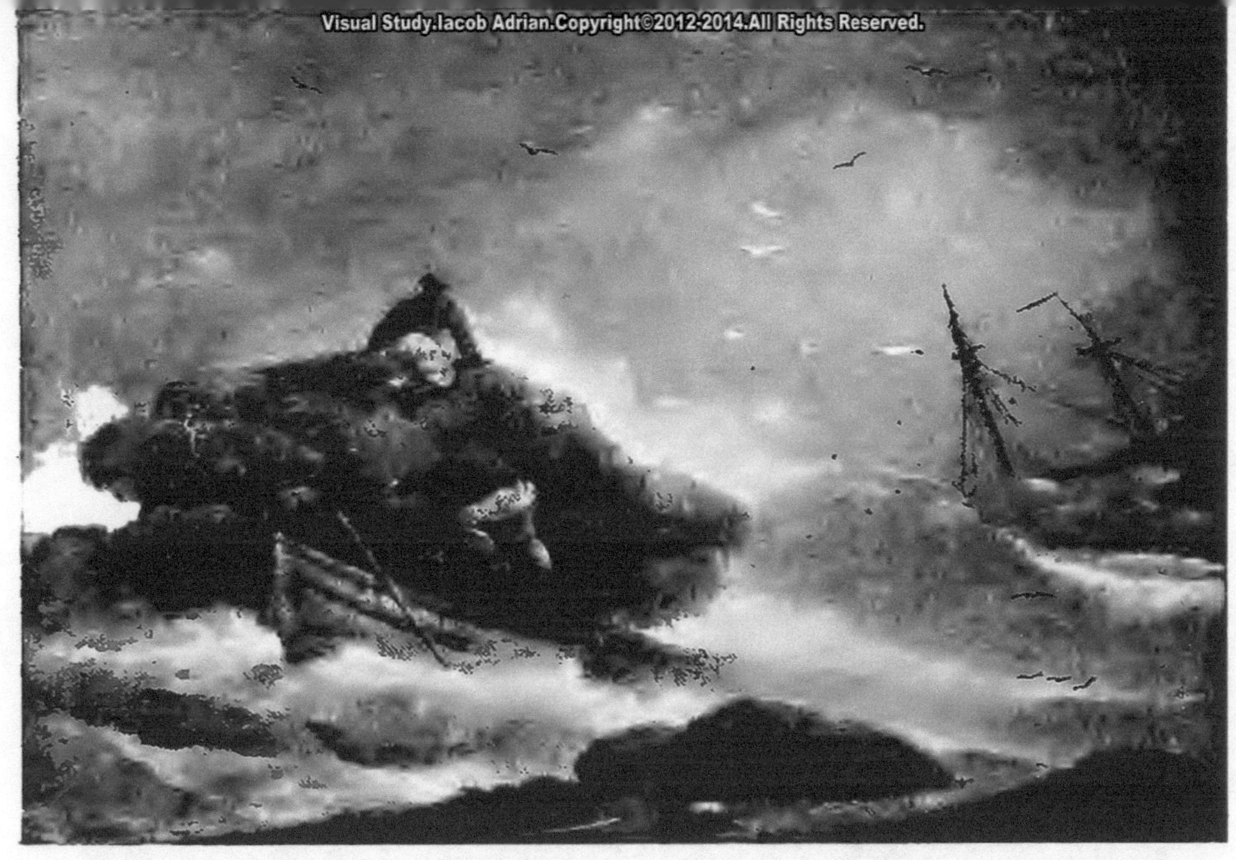

WRECK OF A BOAT SCHIFFBRUCH EINES BOOTES NAUFRAGE D'UN BATEAU

(Mrs. F. Abbiss Phillips, Stoke d'Abernon)

H. Hyatt, Photo.

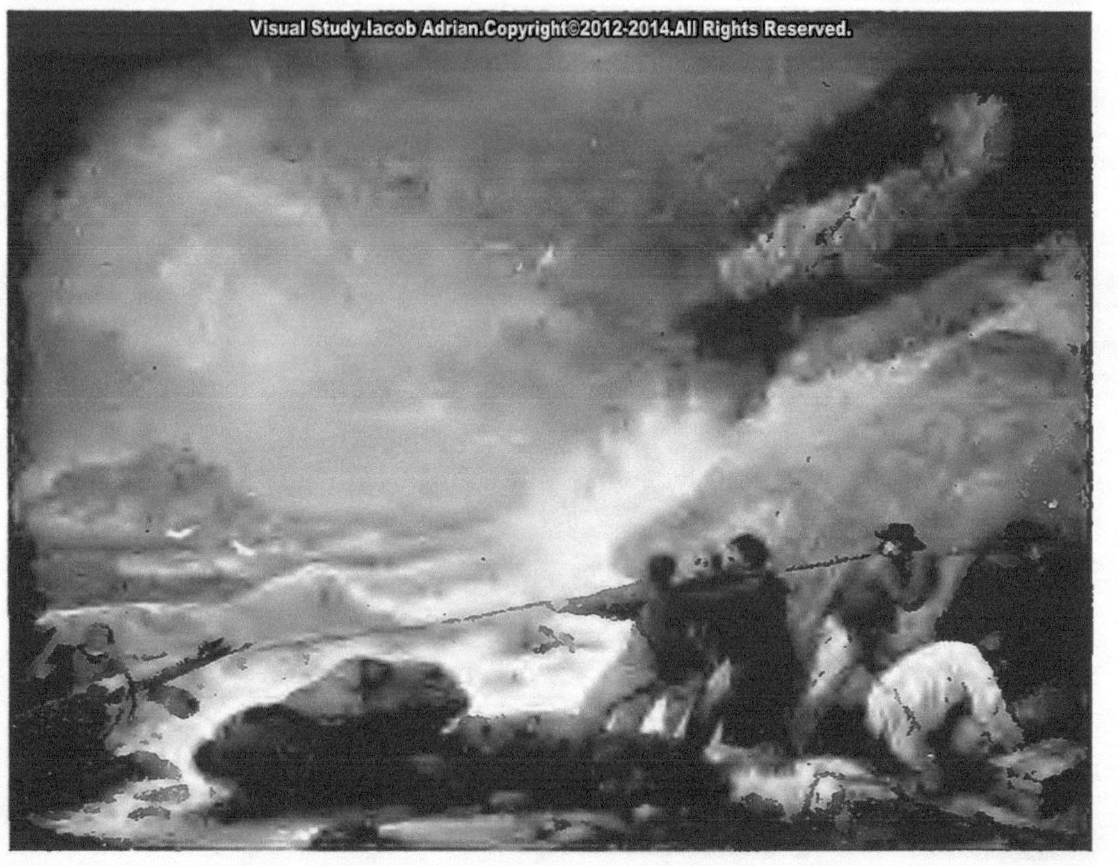

THE DAY AFTER THE WRECK LE LENDEMAIN DU NAUFRAGE

DER TAG NACH DEM SCHIFFBRUCH

(Mrs. F. Abbiss Phillips, Stoke d'Abernon) J. Caswall Smith, Photo.

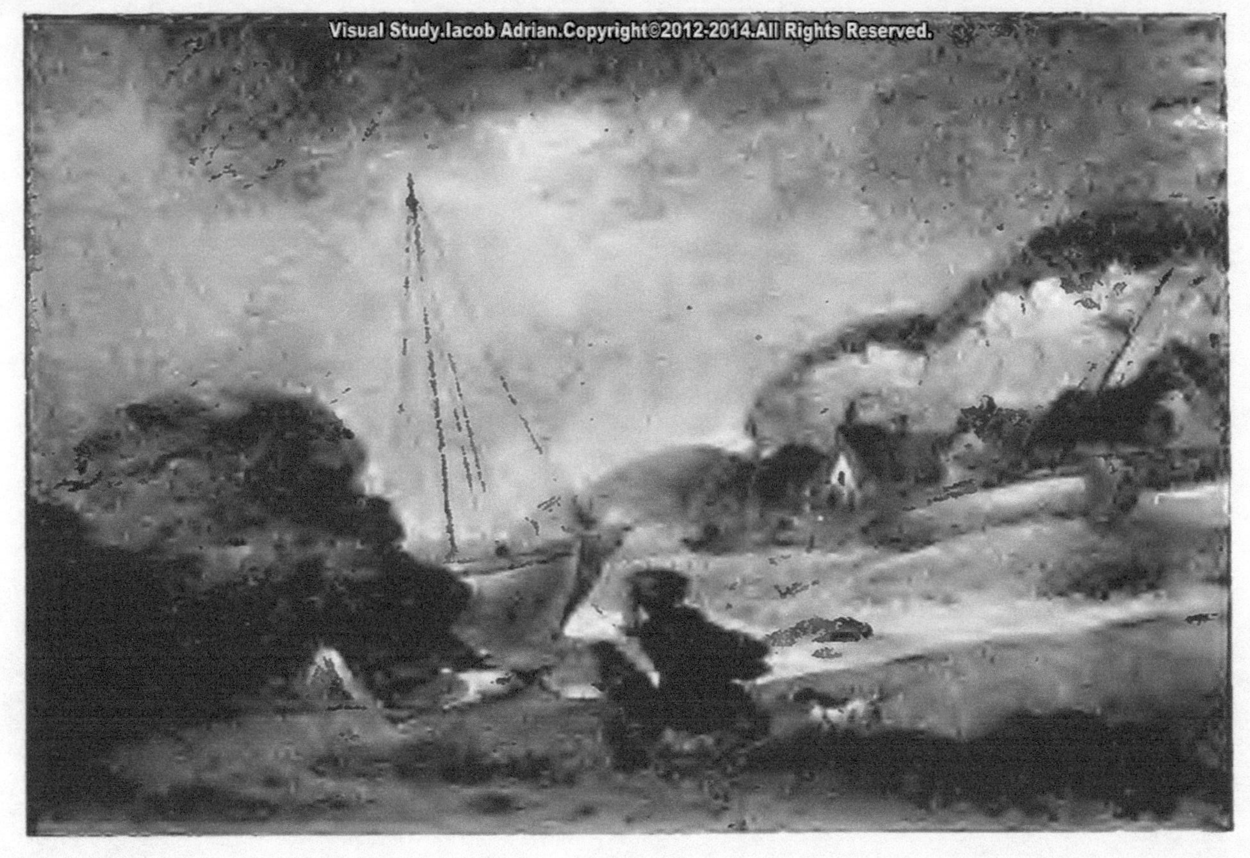

GIRL ON SEASHORE ON WINDY DAY

JEUNE FILLE SUR LA PLAGE PAR UN JOUR DE GRAND VENT

MÄDCHEN AM GESTADE AN EINEM STÜRMISCHEN TAG

(Mrs. F. Abbiss Phillips, Stoke d'Abernon) *J. Caswall Smith, Photo.*

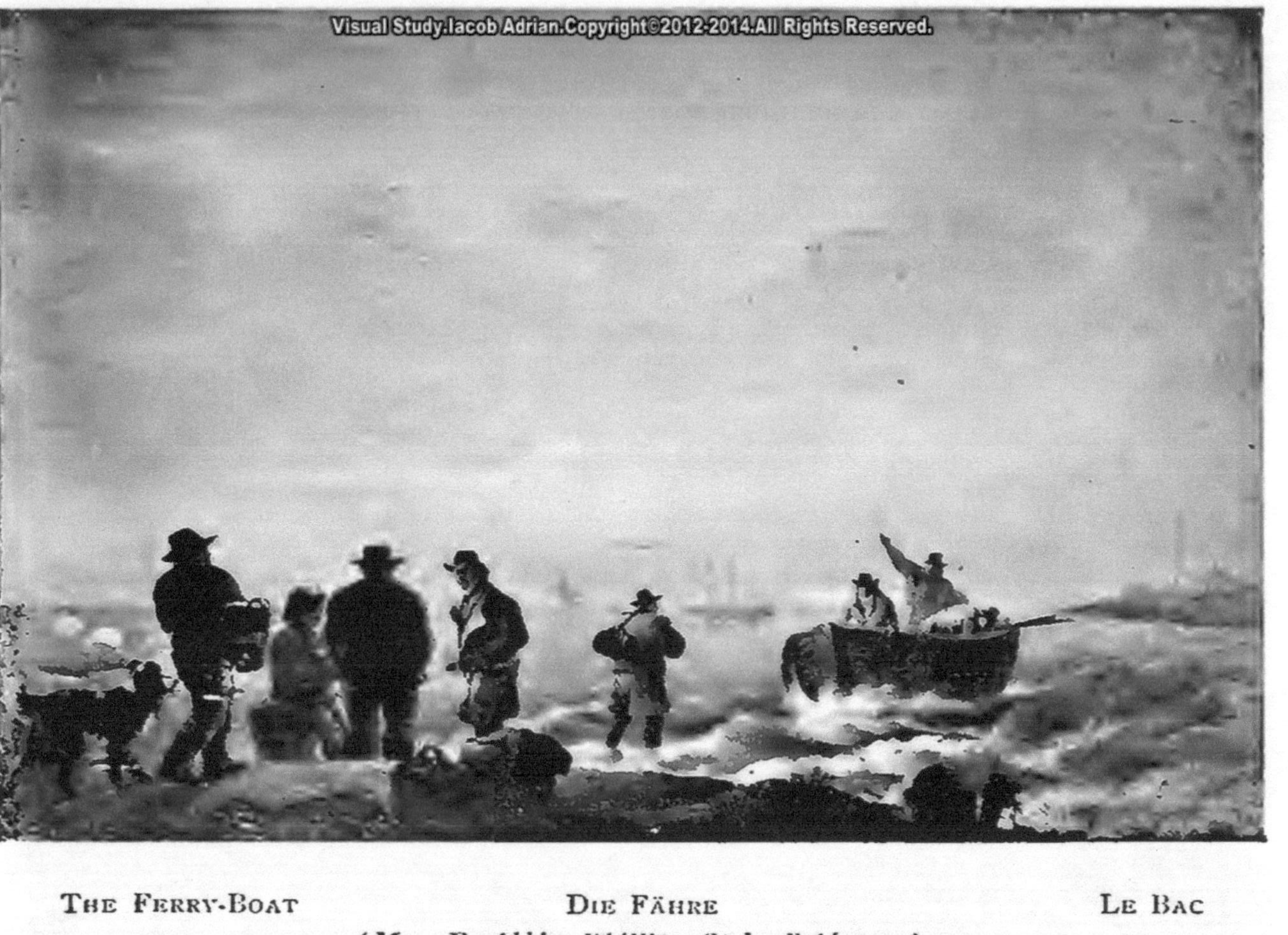

THE FERRY-BOAT DIE FÄHRE LE BAC

(Mrs. F. Abbiss Phillips, Stoke d'Abernon)

J. Caswall Smith, Photo.

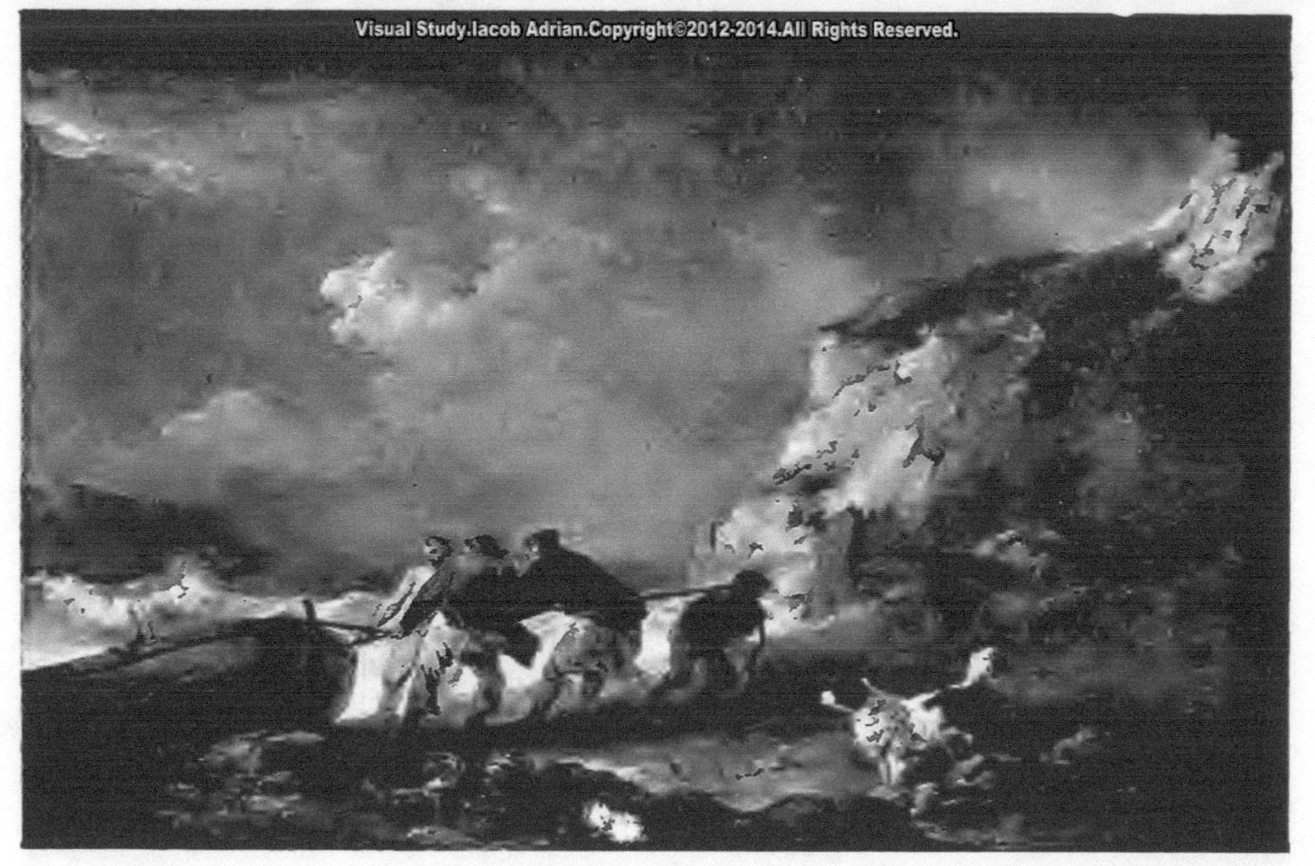

Fishermen hauling in a Boat   Pêcheurs tirant un Bateau a Terre

Fischer ziehen ein Boot an den Strand

(Victoria and Albert Museum, South Kensington)   *W. A. Mansell & Co., Photo.*

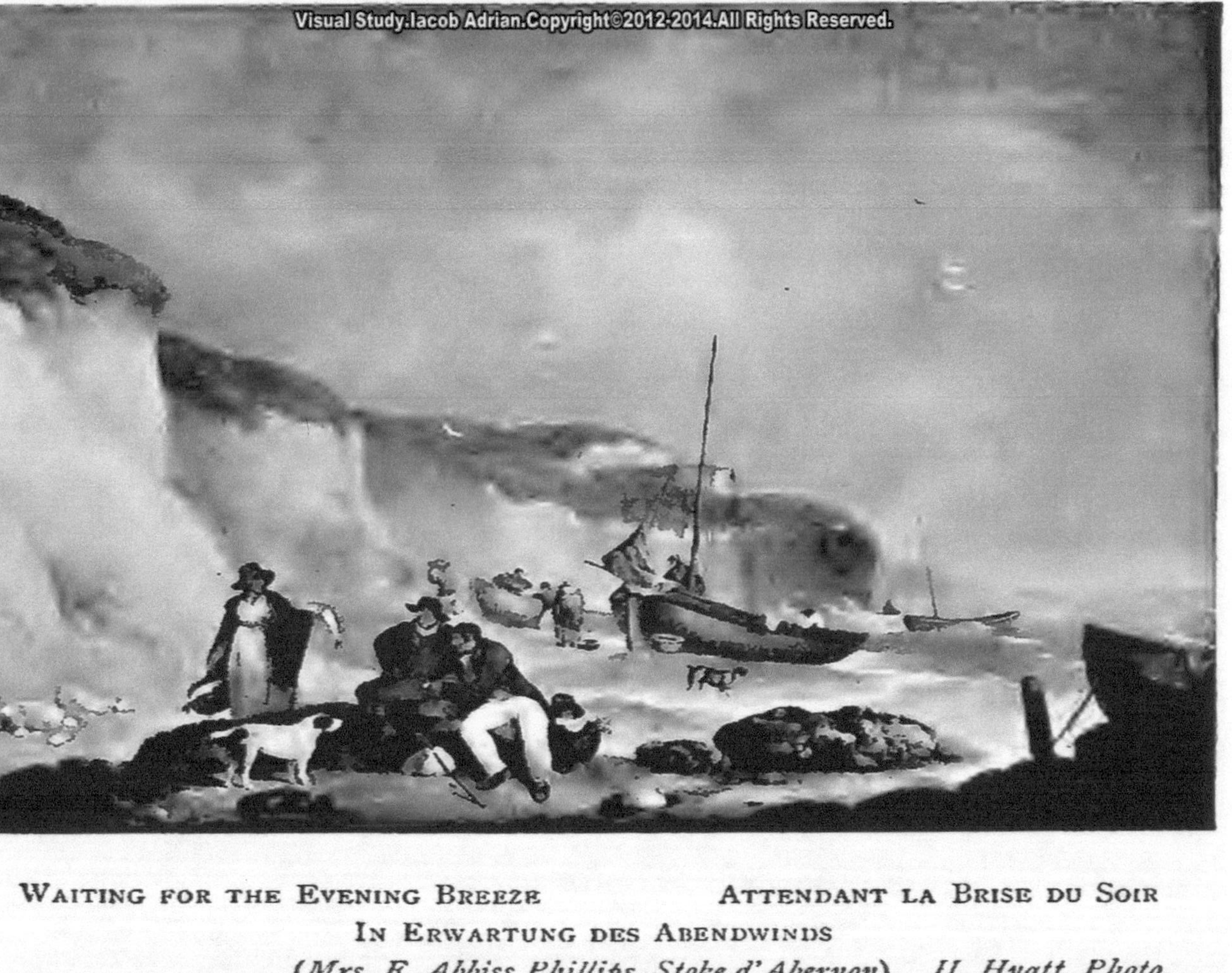

WAITING FOR THE EVENING BREEZE ATTENDANT LA BRISE DU SOIR

IN ERWARTUNG DES ABENDWINDS

(Mrs. F. Abbiss Phillips, Stoke d'Abernon) *H. Hyatt, Photo.*

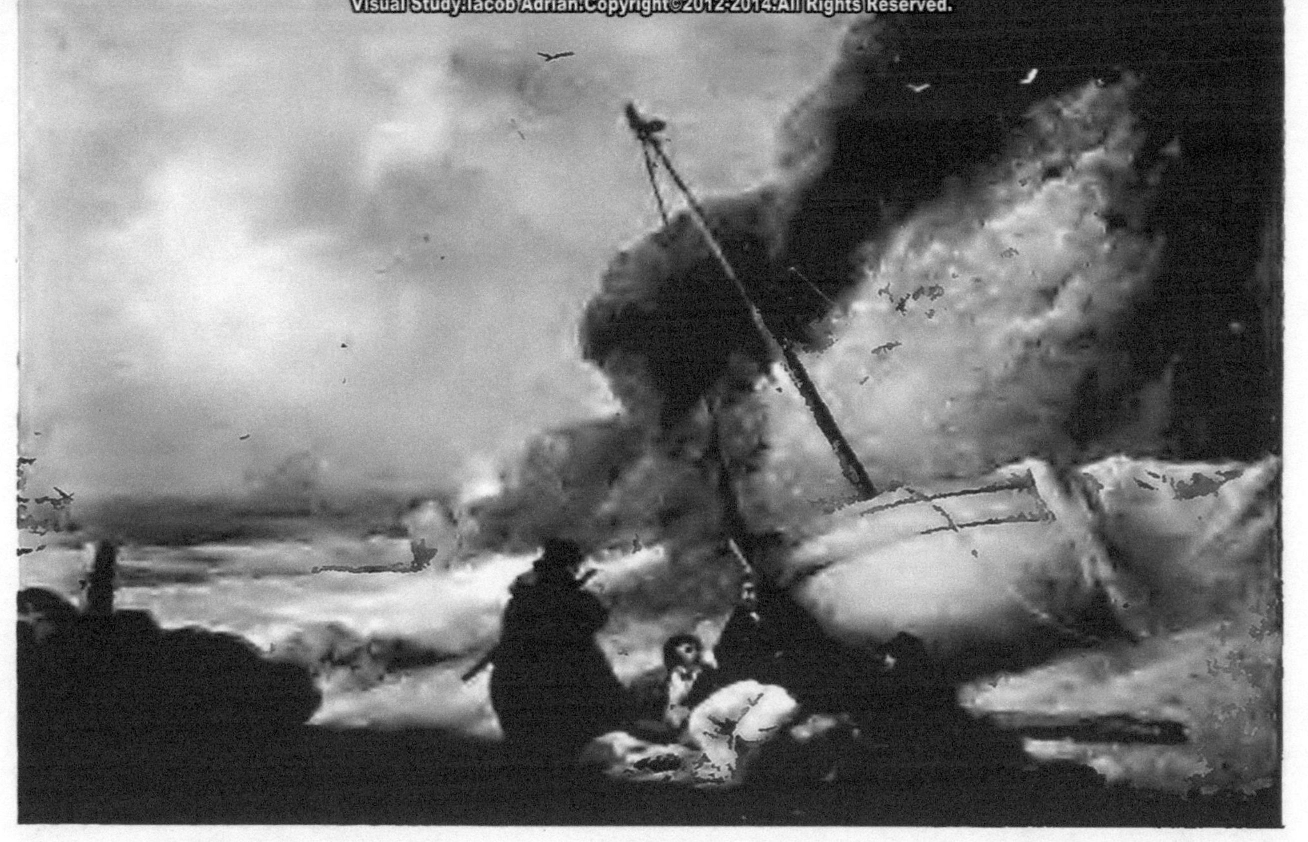

Sea-Coast, Men and Boats — Plage, Hommes et Bateaux

Gestade, Männer und Boote

(Sir Chas. S. Hamilton, London) *J. Caswall Smith, Photo.*

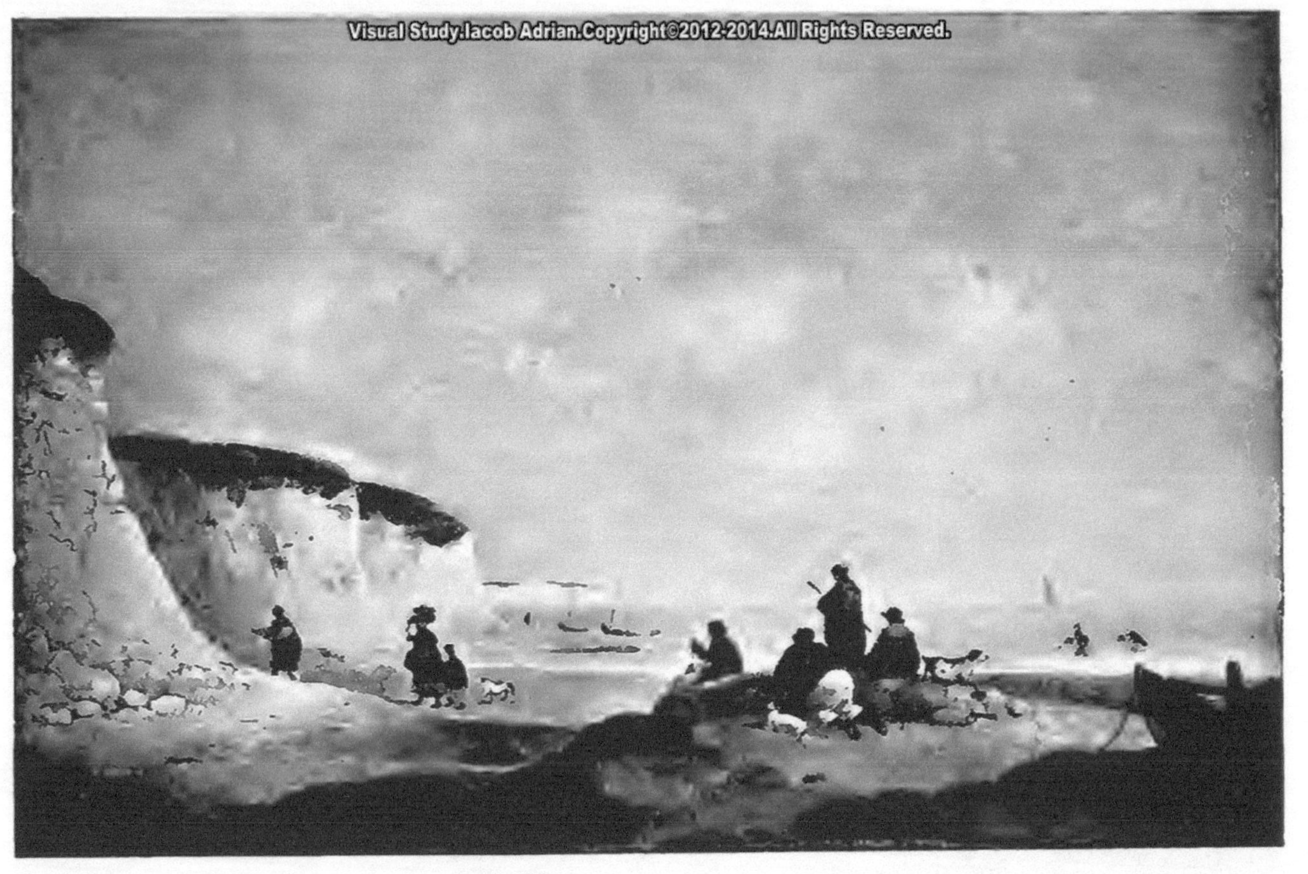

CALM : ISLE OF WIGHT MEERESSTILLE : INSEL WIGHT CALME : ILE DE WIGHT

(Gallery, Leicester)

W. A. Mansell & Co., Photo.

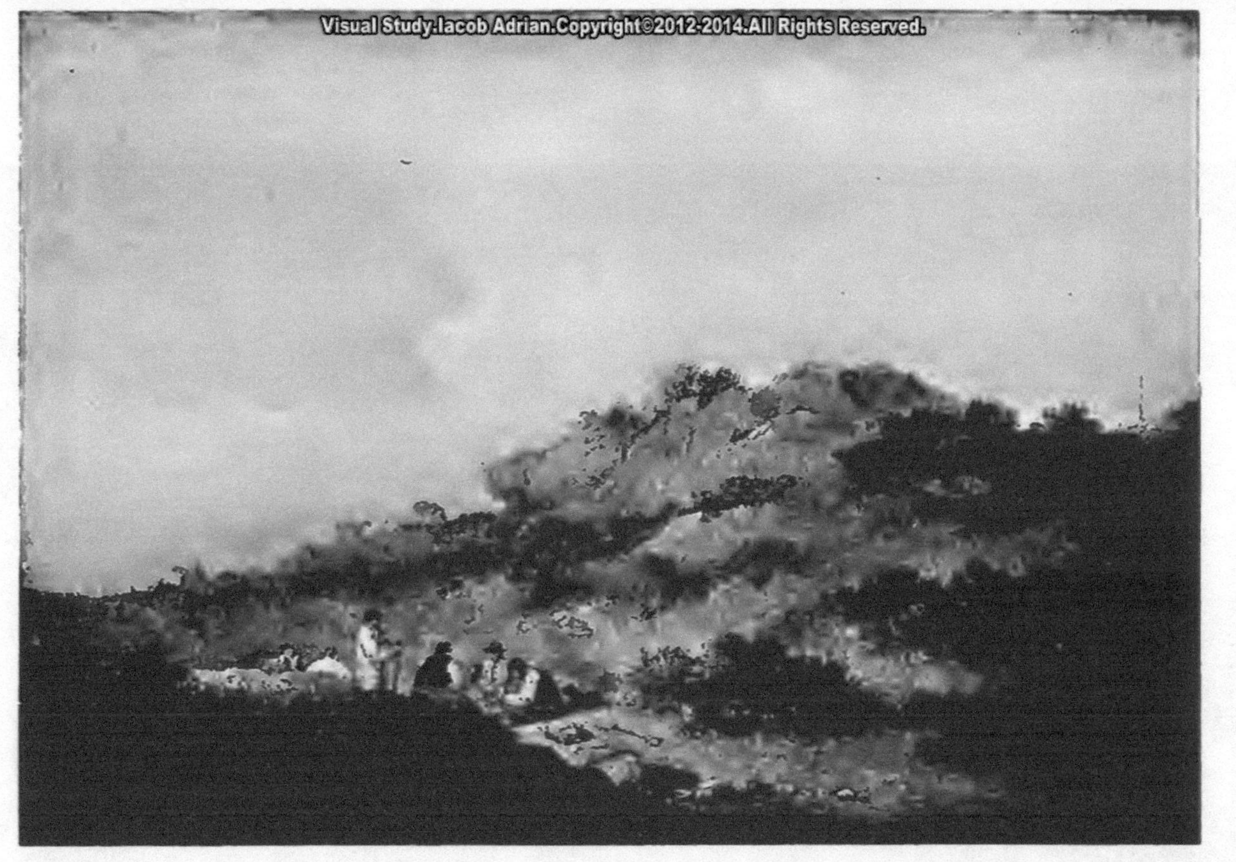

QUARRY, WITH PEASANTS   CARRIÈRE, AVEC DES PAYSANS

STEINBRUCH MIT BAUERN

(National Gallery, London)   *W. A. Mansell & Co., Photo.*

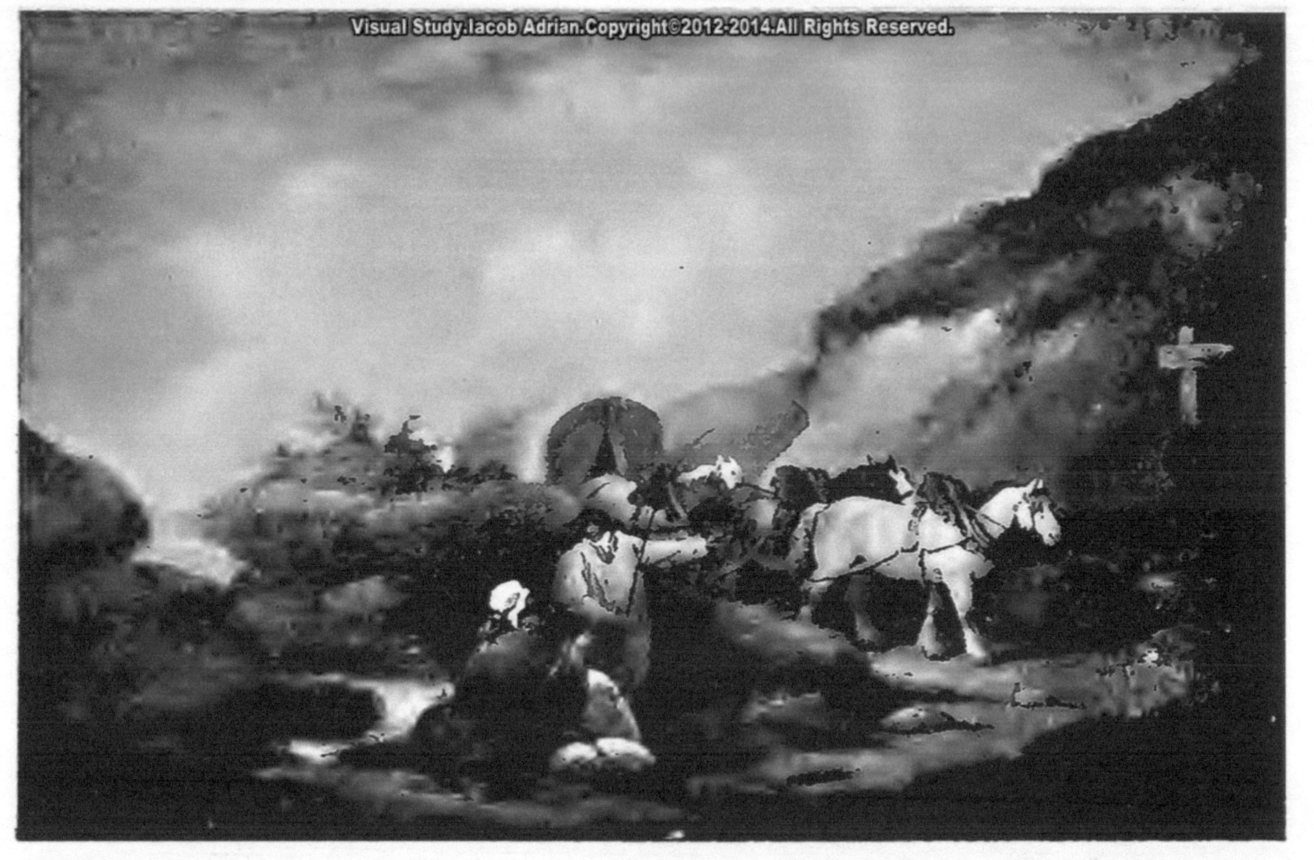

SUMMER SOMMER L'ÉTÉ

(Mrs. F. Abbiss Phillips, Stoke d'Abernon)

H. Hyatt, Photo.

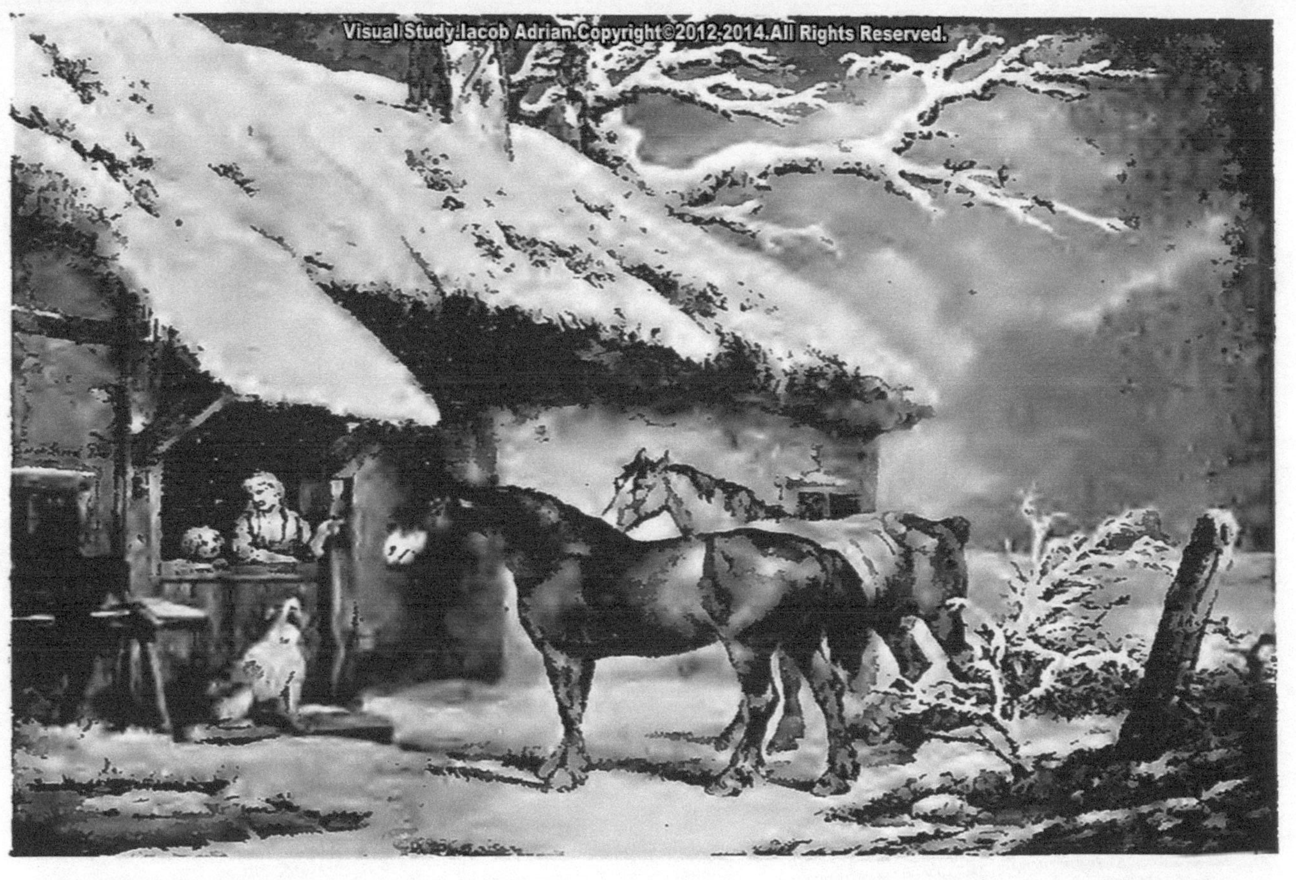

WINTER WINTER L'HIVER

(Mrs. F. Abbiss Phillips, Stoke d'Abernon)

H. Hyatt, Photo.

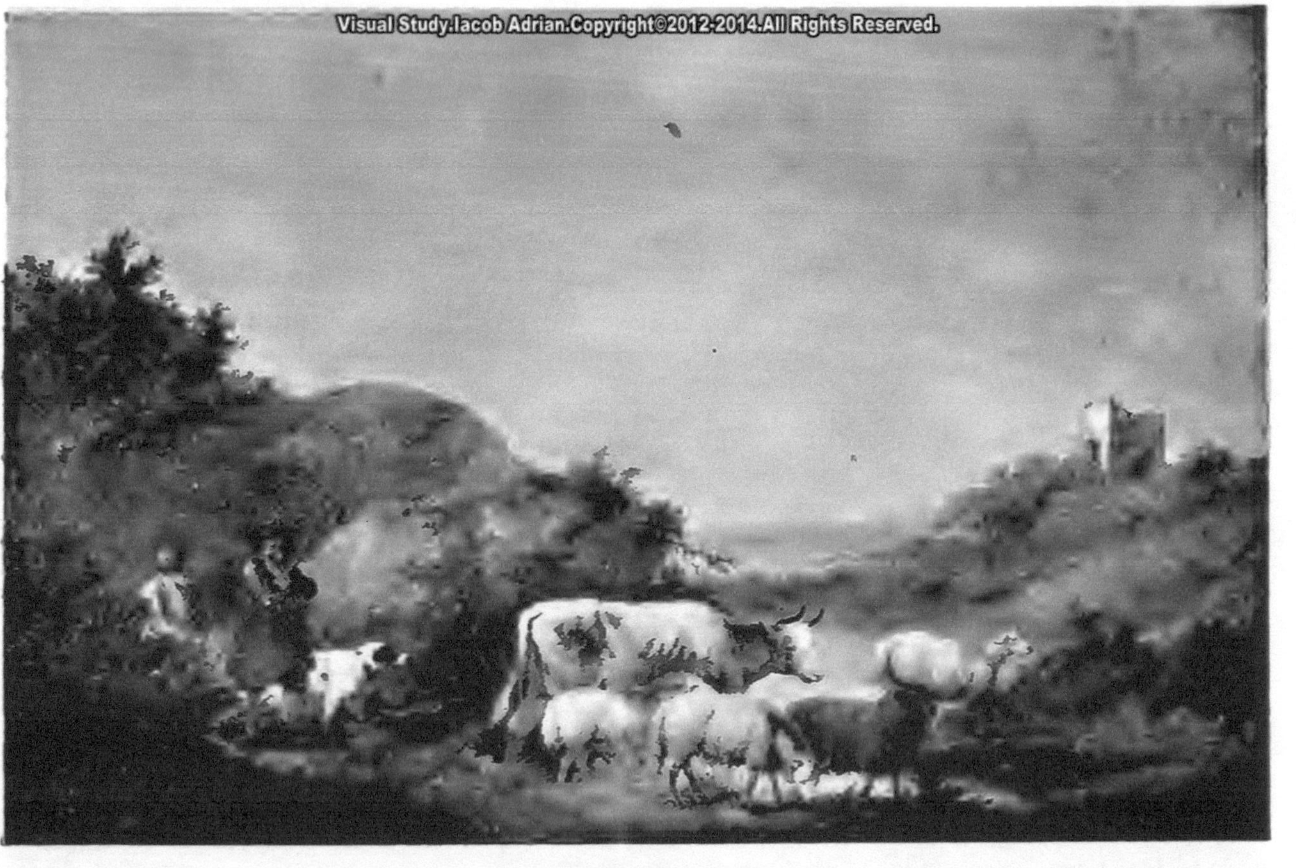

EVENING　　ABEND　　LE SOIR

(*Mrs. F. Abbiss Phillips, Stoke d'Abernon*)

H. Hyatt, Photo.

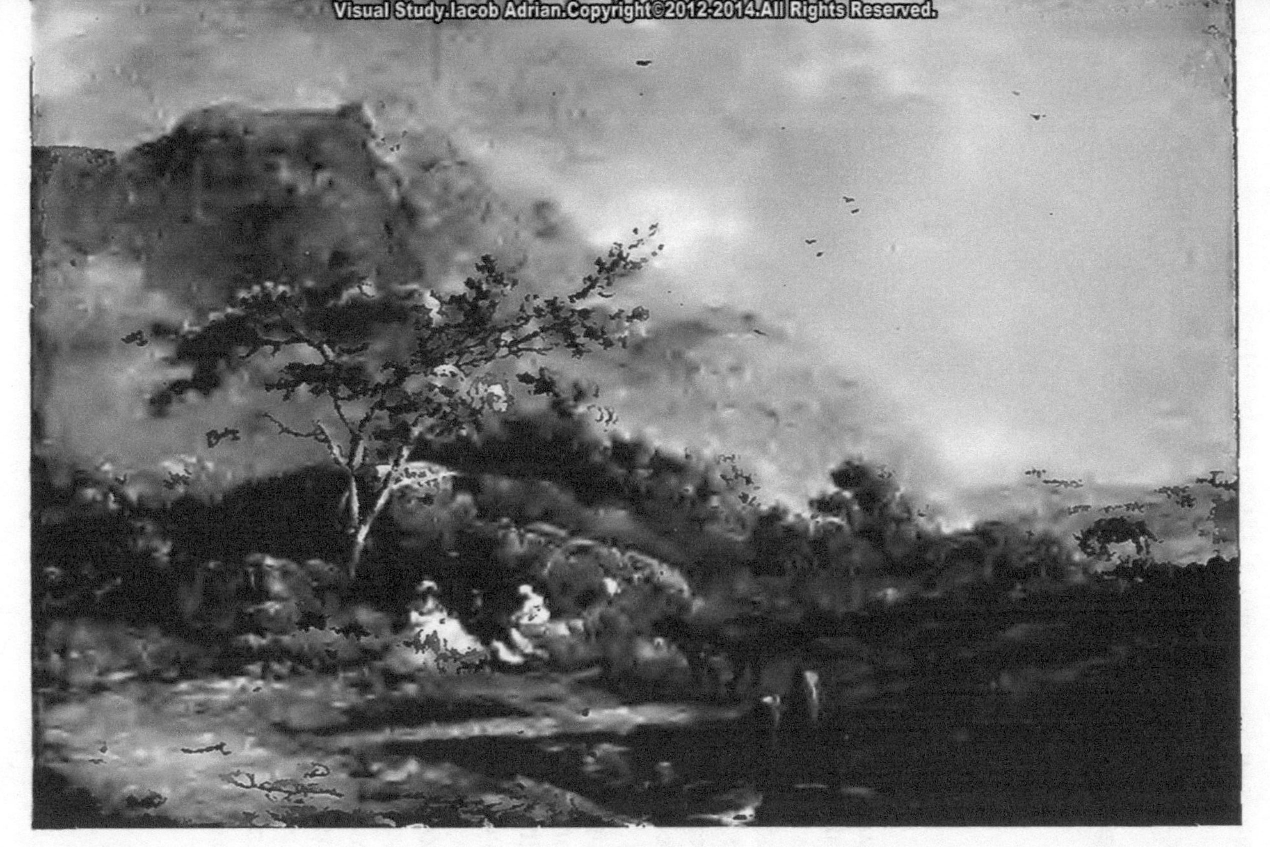

LANDSCAPE LANDSCHAFT PAYSAGE

(Mrs. F. Abbiss Phillips, Stoke d'Abernon)

H. Hyatt, Photo.

Bibliographic sources :

The masterpieces of Morland, 1763-1804 (1911)

Author: Morland, George, 1763-1804

Publisher: London, Gowans & Gray

This documentary study use,
combined in various proportions,
elements from the following categories,
forms and subsets :
- fair use
- documentary
- documentary photography
- feature
- journalism
- arts journalism
- visual journalism
- photojournalism
- celebrity photography

in order to :
- employ material as the object of cultural critique ,
- quote to illustrate an argument or point ,
- use material in historical sequence,

providing independent opinion,
using photos, press articles, advertisements,
opinions of fans etc. ...

www.ingramcontent.com/pod-product-compliance
Lightning Source LLC
Chambersburg PA
CBHW021022180526
45163CB00005B/2070

* 9 7 8 1 5 1 2 3 4 0 1 5 0 *